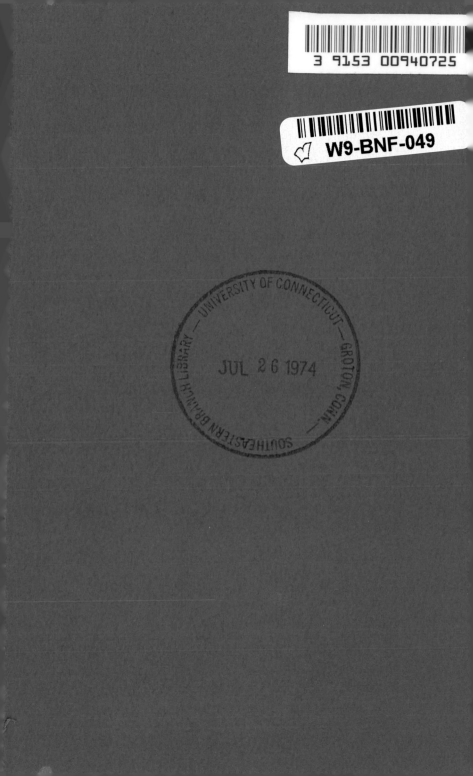

Panthermania

Books by Gail Sheehy

LOVESOUNDS

SPEED IS OF THE ESSENCE

PANTHERMANIA

Panthermania

The Clash of Black Against Black in One American City

GAIL SHEEHY

Harper & Row, Publishers

New York / Evanston / San Francisco / London

A portion of this work appeared in *New York* magazine in somewhat different form.

for Clay

Acknowledgments

I would like to thank Betty and Ernest Osborne for their courage and cooperation in helping me to explore the complexities of a painful experience in their community. There are many other members of the New Haven community whose valuable assistance I can best repay by leaving them nameless. I am especially grateful to William Jones and his son Mentor, who had to be convinced fictitious names would be in their best interest. The only other fictitious name is Walt Johnson, who preferred to remain anonymous.

Finally, I would like to acknowledge the loyalty of David Parks throughout a demanding experiment in interracial journalism; the help of Marilyn Mercer, a *McCall's* editor who planted the first questions in my mind; the research assistance of Jolly Robinson and the support of *New York* editors Jack Nessel, Sheldon Zalaznick, Judith Daniels and especially Clay Felker, who keeps us all honest.

Preface

A year ago I was just as taken up with the Panther cause as anyone else. The country seemed to be out of control and bumbling on all fronts. The war in Southeast Asia was coming back like a fatal leukemia which had fooled us with a short phase of remission. Students were being bullied and killed. The economy was sagging. And perhaps most inexcusable, our meager efforts toward reducing the racial crisis seemed to be at a standstill.

Many of us were tired and shamed by the grotesqueries of justice played out in the Chicago Conspiracy Trial. It had dragged across winter only to end with contempt sentences for the two attorneys and the release of Black Panther Party Chairman Bobby Seale to stand trial in New Haven in connection with the murder of Alex Rackley. It was not an easy time to like anything about the established American system. The only comfort was to identify with heroic rebellions.

During that winter of 1969–1970, I was attending Columbia University on a fellowship in Interracial Reporting. Of all the militant groups fighting against creeping government repression, I thought the most vital and deserving to be the Black Panthers. Before dawn on December 4, 1969, fourteen Chicago policemen attached to the State's Attorney's office executed a reckless and deliberate raid on a Black Panther headquarters. In twelve minutes they left four of the eight Panthers wounded, Fred Hampton, chairman of the Black Panther Party of Illinois, dead, party member Mark Clark dead, and fifty-six bullets and eighty-three empty shells in the apartment. A federal grand jury later traced all but one shell and one shotgun slug to police weapons. With the murder of Fred Hampton I began to think of all Panthers as martyrs.

Revulsion over this incident revived the radical Left. Police conduct associated with the Hampton murder snowballed into a widespread public belief that the government was out to eradicate the Panthers, a conclusion drawn largely from the allegations of one man. Charles Garry, chief counsel and spokesman for the Black Panther Party, told the press that twenty-eight Panthers had been killed by police. He declared that the Chicago raid was part of a national scheme "to destroy and commit genocide upon members of the Black Panther Party." Without verification, Garry's body count passed like gospel throughout the white media. Support mobilized for the beleaguered black revolutionaries in all sorts of nonviolent circles: moderate civil-rights leaders stepped forward; white college presidents, clergymen, politicians and attorneys made statements and the beautiful people created a new social cachet known as the Panther defense fund party.

It was a spellbinding cause. I too rallied, contributed, wore a *Free the Panthers* button. There was only one sacrifice necessary to maintain the comfort of being on the People's side. One could not ask questions.

In April 1970 I was assigned by *New York* magazine to do a piece on reactions of the black community to the Panther trial in New Haven. Twelve men and women assumed to be Black Panthers, including Chairman Bobby Seale, were charged in different degrees with the kidnapping, torture and murder of Alex Rackley, a member of the New York Panther chapter. Bail had been denied except in one case. Those accused had already been in jail for as long as eleven months. It amounted to preventive detention, a "privilege" American courts reserve for the poor and the black. Furthermore, Charles Garry had charged that Rackley was murdered by police agents. Yale students were on strike, demanding that the Panthers awaiting trial be released. A national invitation went out for a May Day rally in defense of the Panthers on the New Haven Green. I was in sympathy with the students and the imprisoned Panthers. But this time I would have to ask questions.

From my girlhood in Connecticut, I had friends in New Haven who knew some of the family members connected with the Panther defendants. I was painfully aware of my own handicaps as a reporter: my whiteness, of course, but also my sympathy with the black radical cause. This story needed the balance of a black point of view. I called on David Parks, a young black photographer who had also written a book, *GI Diary.* And so we set out on the first of May, 1970, on what was to be a short experiment in interracial journalism. We finished nine months later.

The first few days in New Haven we camped on the floor of Yale Medical Center. One by one we met black community advocates who gave us statements not to be quoted and names to contact on our own. We sought out friends and families of the Panther defendants. Some refused to see us, most were friendly but guarded. They all quizzed us on our own attitudes. With our primary informants we pledged not to publish a story before submitting the manuscript to them and their lawyers.

We half lived in New Haven throughout that summer. It was a schizophrenic experience. We stayed with white friends and crossed lines each day to eat with, rap with and learn from new black friends. Throughout the Lonnie McLucas trial, which would set the pattern for the other defendants, we kept in close touch. State and court officials gave us their side but nothing was for attribution. A court order had been passed prohibiting "extra-judicial statements" by anyone connected with the trial. I tried to purchase a transcript of the pretrial testimony and was stalled for two months, until one day I chased the court reporter down the marble steps of New Haven Superior Courthouse for an answer. The judge subsequently ruled no transcripts would be released until the last defendant had been sentenced.

The story would not finish itself. Ramifications of the present Panther experience and its influence on this one city extended way back into the decade of urban renewal and related to the other events which were producing Panther fever across the nation. We watched the white radical movement go through its predictable rituals, united in its commitment not to pursue the facts. Both David and I were astonished at how little we had known about what we had blithely defended in the name of black progress. It was a lonely time.

Writing the story was slow and painful, as I fought with myself about the purpose in publishing bad news about any black people. A lesson from my newspapering days came back to me: Sooner or later truth comes to the surface. If all the bleeding heart white liberals kept silent until the Panther myth came apart of its own accord, wouldn't the black community at large have to take the blame? And so I continued to ask questions and found that the levels of opinion within the black community were many—not one; and that the short article I was writing had become a book.

The actions surrounding the murder of Alex Rackley, although described in a novelistic style, are only those corroborated by court testimony of two or more participants in the events and confirmed by the accounts of community members and public officials. Where the action is in dispute, the conflict is so noted.

At this writing the trial of Bobby Seale and Ericka Huggins on capital charges is under way. A jury has been painstakingly drawn from 1,550 persons called for questioning over four months. Assemblage of the five blacks and seven whites took longer than any other jury selection in the state and surpassed the record 1,400-man venire called in the trial of New Orleans businessman Clay Shaw, who was acquitted of conspiring to assassinate President Kennedy. Both Bobby Seale and Ericka Huggins are charged with aiding and abetting murder, kidnapping resulting in death, and conspiracy to murder and to kidnap. Added to Mrs. Huggins' charges is "binding with intent to commit a crime."

Trial proceedings will again coincide with the annual spring rites of campus protest. And protest is a healthy thing. I would only hope that this year we all have more courage to consult the facts and to resist the emotional catharsis of manufacturing black martyrs. There is too much real work to be done.

New York   G.S.
March 1971

Panther. . .   Revolution is a glorious term, it's a term to be proud of, and we should know—that we are morally right . . . and that the oppressor has no rights which the oppressed are bound to respect.

—Eldridge Cleaver, *Minister of Information, Black Panther Party*

Mania. . .   Excessive excitement or enthusiasm; craze. (Psychiatry) A form of insanity characterized by great excitement, with or without delusions, and in its acute stage by great violence.

—Random House Dictionary

How the hell do you even know they're Panthers? It sounds to me like you've got a bad case of Panthermania.

—Betty Kimbro Osborne to her brother, Warren Kimbro, *New Haven, March, 1969*

Panthermania

1

WE WENT TO New Haven believing. Bread and circuses were breaking out all over Yale to celebrate the town's first Black Panther rally. It was May Day, 1970, and the pitch of protest was at an emotional high. With the murder of Fred Hampton still fresh in mind, with Panther-baiting on the rise at home and the invasion of Cambodia a bitter truth abroad (though at that point unacknowledged), one had to take sides.

Nine Panthers were in prison in Connecticut. They were charged with conspiring to kidnap and murder Alex Rackley, another party member. Two more Panthers were fighting extradition from Denver, Colorado, in connection with the killing. White students and racist-fighting faculty had boiled the case down to the simplicity of a page from a Dick and Jane book.

Fifteen thousand of us on the New Haven Green, and uncounted thousands across the country, swallowed the conventional wisdom uncritically: the Panthers were being framed. The state was railroading them into a trial for the murder of a police informer, organized by another police informer, and pinned on party Chairman Bobby Seale. Therefore police were the criminals. The issue was political freedom. The trial was just another trick bag into which white people are constantly putting black people.

Even the president of Yale, for his own purposes, confirmed our belief that a black revolutionary could not receive a fair trial in America.

One fact kept tugging at the back of my mind. *A real murder had been committed and two men had already confessed to it.* I was having trouble dismissing murder as nothing more than politics.

But Tom Hayden was right there exhorting us to ignore the facts. "In Huey Newton's trial the first thing people wanted to know was the *facts* of the case," said the chief theorist of the New Left with scorn. "The hardest thing is to convince them the facts are irrelevant." Hayden was again hailed as the most creative thinker within mass-protest politics. He finished off by proclaiming Bobby Seale's trial "the most important trial of a black man in American history." *Why then, I wondered, aren't the black people of New Haven out on the Green united in a chorus of "Right ons"?*

My first clue came when I heard a local black marshal roar angrily through a bullhorn at a black militant from Harvard who was jeering police. "Hold it, brother!" the local man shouted. "When you go home we got to live here!"

On the second day of reporting I hit a giant snag. A local black family described the events leading up to the Rackley killing. They were related to one of the confessed triggermen. Almost nothing in their account squared with the sloganeering going on around the Green.

David Parks, the black photographer, and I circulated a little further. We spent Saturday morning on Dixwell Avenue rapping with young dudes outside the Soul Center and wise old women on the benches of the laundromat. After the rally we drove out to the black marshal's home in suburban Hamden, and on to dinner with a reasonable white university family I knew well. No one thought for a moment the Panthers were being framed. They seriously wondered how many of the people involved in the Rackley killing were even Panthers. What was a Panther anyway?

I was confounded. Thousands of Panther supporters were coming together voluntarily to listen only to each other, and were thinking with one mass propagandized mind. They had all but brought a great university to its knees. Why were the simplest facts of the case being ignored? How much authenticity did the Panthers have as spokesmen for their own people? How much did *any* of us know about the true nature of the Panther party?

The answers were important because the most astonishing distortion of free political thought was under way right out there on the Green. One thing was very clear: New Haven was in the grip of Panther fever.

Brigades of white Panthers, it was promised at the rally, would return for the summer to liberate New England. But after May Day weekend the exhilarated white radicals went back to their colleges or homes. Feeling incomplete, David Parks and I stayed around town awhile. We were in and out of New Haven during the next six months, slowly making friends and sharing moments of crisis and weeks of normality with New Haveners. The real story of the Panther trial

GAIL SHEEHY

drifted away from Bobby Seale. It belonged to the black community.

In New Haven as late as 1968 the Panther party was still considered a mysterious aberration of California-style nut politics. New Haven is nothing like Los Angeles or Oakland. The city of perpetual new beginnings, the capital of quick-frozen American superculture, Los Angeles is a natural attraction for fanatics and freak politicians of all stripes. Oakland is the training center for revolutionary gamesmanship and much better at it than any East Coast city.

Nor is New Haven anything like New York, which has always drawn people to its mystery and danger and energy. Chicago, Second City, knows bloodshed so well that a showdown between cops and Panthers there came as second nature. Detroit, Atlanta, even Philadelphia was a more likely spot for black militancy to explode. But it was in New Haven that the Panther movement finally lost its innocence.

New Haven is Third City, U.S.A. Solid, dull, but indisputably stable. Like hundreds of our third cities, its face is kept powdered though its innards may be arthritic. Above all, it does not complain outside the family.

Sited on a plain and ridged with mildly knuckled hills, New Haven is not quite on yachty Long Island Sound, not really part of hard-nosed Naugatuck Valley life, and estranged from New York by its more fashionable cousin to the south, Fairfield County. Only after an extended rivalry with Hartford did New Haven settle for being nicknamed the "semicapital" of Connecticut.

Eventually New Haven made its own way on the skirts of

Yale. Its hub is Yale and her Beaux Arts Gothic towers trimmed in stone ribbons and gargoyles. Yale's New Haven is aloof and aristocratic, occupied with pursuits of the mind. From Yale and the central Green the city spreads in a wheel-spoke design through seven inner-city black neighborhoods which liberals have done their best to "renew," whitewash and suburbanize into just-like-us acquiescence. Immediately outside this inner city the spokes end. Semiprofessional bedroom towns spread up the hilly ridges where affluent suburbanites tuck themselves in after dark. From there the escape routes of the last decade spill out to shore towns of ferocious Italian and Irish ethnic vanity.

The art of high provincialism is commonly practiced in New Haven, but not without a certain puritanical pride. Residents keep abreast on the rumor pump. There is a black grapevine and a network of ethnic white grapevines and then the academic community, which attempts to monitor the appropriate grapevine only when the ignored residents of central New Haven blow the lid off the town.

The fuse of such an explosion was lit in January of 1969 by the funeral of John Huggins, New Haven's first native Black Panther. Four months later the Panther party burned out in Connecticut. Plagued by its own inexperience and internal paranoia, the party went through a standardized chain of events: (1) murder of a suspected informer, (2) police raid and (3) Panther trial.

But the scars would not heal. The fires lit in the imagination of young black minds would not burn out. Ignited and reignited by clashes around the country, these small painful fires, concealed inside the brightest of adolescent minds, smoldered on until it became evident to the black community at large that some new and unquenchable force was taking their young, pulling them together in a far left corner of the national black forest which they itched to defend . . . and that New Haven was a false boundary.

The state of the Panther party in any town at any particular time during 1970 did not really matter, because the fever had passed to the children. At its peak Panther fever bestowed dignity on the black man. It sent shudders through the white man. And the irony is that J. Edgar Hoover may have been the nation's greatest Panther recruiter. Who could have imagined he would label the few dozen men and women who were the Panthers in 1968 the greatest threat to the internal security of the United States? What a challenge to live up to!

The revolutionary life style requires battlefront reflexes, gut responses. It can be strong enough even to pull a lost man-child back from the traditional comfort of dope. The pace is right. The demands of urban guerrilla life offer a substitute for the desperate but habitual rhythm of hustling, which is the hardest thing for an addict to give up. In fact, the demands of urban guerrilla life are greater. Consider also the lure of mobility. Revolutionaries travel—planes, cabs, Chicago, Detroit, California, Cuba, Hanoi, Algiers—moving with the spontaneity of the jet set and the mystery of the Mafia, all financed by adoring white liberals and dignified by a noble cause. Imagine the prospect as seen by a boy raised in front of the bedroom TV with a house key around his neck, marking time among the shut-ins of the ghetto. Even his parents can see the pull. It extends past party lines and trial names. A certain psychopolitical hope had caught the imagination of black children and was burning like a billion wooden matches struck in unison across the emotions.

Outside New Haven the whole phenomenon went by the name Bobby Seale, or the Bobby Seale trial. Inside black New Haven, where doors are tight and the furies kept private and families think first of their own flesh and blood, it became known as Panthermania.

The strain of Panthermania weighed most heavily on the black middle class. Ties between the old Toms and young militants had already been severed by the end of the civil-rights era. But now a clash between middle-class values and black radicalism—and even more internal and ferocious, the clash between Panthers and black nationalist groups—began tearing at the heart of America's black community. It was destroying as many people as the shoot-outs between cops and militants. As the tense seventies began, the most uncomfortable spot in America may have been in the black middle.

The new black politicians, suburbanites, bus children and button-down parents . . . the reviled black cops and leftover civil rightsers caught in a tragic shift . . . the antipoverty workers and college liaisons and community advocates belonging to a new professional class . . . the first-mortgage holders and franchise operators who cashed in on the fleeting opportunities of black capitalism . . . the ambivalent doctor, lawyer, college professor and their wives, home at last, with their Afros set carefully in curlers—the whole spectrum of middle-class upward-mobile black America was caught in a bind.

With the middle beleaguered and fading, the choice was

grim. Americans in the black middle stood between the Hoover-Agnew people, who threatened to take away freedoms so recently gained, and the Cleaver-Hoffman people, who gave as the sane alternative "revolutionary suicide." Many were with the Panther program in spirit. But in practice the Panthers brought tragedy.

In the three years since Huey P. Newton's two columns of fiercely armed black men marched into California's state capitol building—etching forever on the stunned consciousness of America the image of black foot soldiers arrayed in berets, cartridge belts, M-1 rifles and twelve-gauge shotguns and demanding the right to bear arms in self-defense—the bloodshed has been all the more bitter because no one counts the bodies the same way. According to Justice Department records in November of 1970, the tally stood: 469 black people assumed to be Panthers have been arrested; ten Panthers and eleven police officers have been shot dead. According to Panther estimates, their death toll has been much higher. Whatever the actual body count, Panther deaths have been tallied, retallied and distorted out of all proportion to the party's actual membership. This is because the Panther movement was created by and for the media. The more it was publicized by the liberal white media, the greater the imagined ranks of a black army grew. This gave police a massive case of Pantherphobia. And a good excuse to attack.

While the police and FBI spread the myth of open warfare between cops and Panthers, defenders of the movement backed up the myth. Attorney Charles Garry (following the Fred Hampton murder in December 1969) gave the statement that twenty-eight Panthers had been killed by police.

This was accepted as the official body count by the media. It was repeated everywhere from *Time* to *The New York Times* and over the television newscasts without question.

But included in Garry's figures were ten men who died either in shoot-outs with rival black militants belonging to the separatist black organization US (John Huggins and Bunchy Carter in Los Angeles; John Savage and Sylvester Bell in San Diego), or by Panther members or by a gun registered in a Panther's name (Alex Rackley in New Haven; Frank Diggs in Los Angeles). Two of the others were killed during robbery attempts by the civilians they held up. Another presumed Panther died from an overdose of barbiturates. And still another of the victims included in Garry's count made his own dying declaration: in a domestic quarrel, Nathaniel Clark was shot by his wife.

All of this might have paled before the death toll among Chicago's rival youth gangs had the media not been preoccupied with the Panthers. In Chicago black children of the high-rise housing projects are locked in lethal combat *with each other*. Each gang—the Black P-Stone Nation, Deuces Wild, Cobrastone and dozens of others—holds its own project building by terror. In the first nine months of 1970 the victims of youth-gang-related shootings numbered 699! Almost all of them were young blacks. Sixty-four of the victims died and twelve police officers were killed during the same period. But these young people are nonpolitical. And youth gangs are an old story. The media need more than a string of routine homicides to become interested in black deaths.

Achievements, yes. The Panthers made visible the sins of our legal system; the traditions of lengthy pretrial detention and proportionately the highest bail set for our poorest people; and the intolerable conditions in our prisons. But at the same time the Panther cause was taking a painful, unmeasured toll: it was pulling the rug out from under a mobilized but still unstable middle class.

There was an especially tragic aspect to Panthermania reaching its climax in New Haven. This was the Model City, bellwether for the nation in urban redevelopment. Out of New Haven came the magic phrases "human renewal" and "people programs." Into New Haven poured more federal and private money per capita for a longer period of time than anywhere else in the country. When Washington's commitment to save the cities peaked in the mid-sixties, New Haven was estimated to be drawing federal urban-renewal allocations of $790 for every woman, man and child.

Black New Haven sat a very long time while white liberals spoke for them. Since 1958 city fathers had run their bulldozers over New Haven's inner-city neighborhoods. For twelve years bulldozers ate up the ugliness and plowed under the obvious. By the time black people woke up, downtown New Haven was already gone. Removed. To be renewed. Dust soup.

Five thousand living units were demolished between 1954 and 1966. A scant 1,500 units replaced them. Of these, almost half were assigned to middle-income and elderly New Haveners, while 793 were luxury housing. Only twelve public-housing units were designed for low-income people!

Where tacky bars and derelict frame houses went down, sweeping people away with them, a supermarket of architectural wonders went up. Mayor Richard Lee, working with

Yale for political mileage, sought the biggest names in architecture. The city lavished design excellence on such projects as a rubber-company headquarters by Marcel Breuer; an international Knights of Columbus headquarters by Kevin Roche; Philip Johnson's new virus laboratory for Yale; and Eero Saarinen's skating rink, which looked more like a display case for the whale-sized ego. To this was added a bright new Monopoly board of office buildings, stores, a hotel and the highways to reach them. The centerpiece was laid in place by Paul Rudolph. New Haven's most proudly offered example of rebirth was Rudolph's 1,380-car parking garage. It was a fair example of urban redevelopment in America; to quote resident architectural scholar Vincent Scully, it was "cataclysmic, automotive and suburban."

Seldom had so much money and talent and time and hope been brought to bear on the ills of a contemporary American city. If urban revival was going to work, it should have worked in New Haven.

It didn't. In 1967 New Haven had a ghetto riot. By 1968 the exodus of dispirited talent was nearly complete. Richard Nixon entered the scene and made it abruptly clear that the grand experiment in citizen participation had had its decade in the sun.

Americans seemed exhausted. Faith had lapsed in government, in the ability of the lifeless, octopean arms of technocracy ever to embrace and respond to people problems. Politics was losing the people, white as well as black.

2

NEW HAVEN FIRST DISCOVERED it had a Panther in the family when John Huggins' dead body came home from California. By then, however, the tragic course of Panthermania was well into an advanced stage.

John Huggins came out of a Negro tradition that goes way back in Connecticut. Around New Haven he was known as the prodigal son of one of the oldest-line black bourgeois families. He attended Hopkins Grammar, an exclusive private boys' school in New Haven. His home, a sedate brick five-bedroom colonial, was the envy of his few black friends. The acre of play yard spread around it beckoned lots of children from Hillhouse High School, which was just down the street. And when John attended Hillhouse, most of the friends he brought home were white. Dixwell Avenue was two blocks away. Dixwell is the oldest and largest black ghetto in New Haven. But ghetto life scarcely touched John Huggins before his twentieth birthday.

His room bulged with three hundred books. His mother worked at Yale's Sterling Library. Everyone respected his father, a formidable patriarch with finely groomed hair, because he followed the traditional route to success in New Haven. Today it may be ridiculed as the house-folk route. But prior to the sixties it was practically the only path to respectability for black people in New England.

John Huggins, Sr., manages the Fence Club. The exclusivity of this Yale social society has been forty years under his iron guardianship. His name is hammered deep into the brass nameplate outside its ivy-trimmed door: JOHN HUGGINS, PERMITTEE—reminiscent of a more exclusive heyday which Mr. Huggins mourns. But Yale masters and students of untarnished Anglo-Saxon heritage still gather at the Fence to drink and dine in the heavy oak Great Hall manner of medieval English kings.

Respect for patina rubbed off on John Huggins, Sr., and he passed it on to his children. Reserved, temperate, academically inclined, the Hugginses were considered, by whites, proper in their place. Black families envied them.

One of John's friends, who came up the hard way through welfare and the projects and today attends medical school at Yale, remembers his childhood picture of the Hugginses. "They were a together black family, living 'decent' up near the good high school. They were all devout parishioners of Dixwell Avenue Congregational Church or Saint Luke's Episcopal." John Huggins taught his friend to daydream white.

"We'd hike about fifteen miles out to Sleeping Giant Park," recalls Walt Johnson. "There's an old castle on top of the mountain and this was our domain. Every Saturday we'd pack a lunch and climb the mountain to eat in the castle. We pretended we were knights in shining armor and the castle was in sixteenth-century England. The other Boy Scouts we took along were our court." (Walt Johnson later felt sheepish about recounting their dreams: "It would probably surprise most white people what goes through a black boy's mind.")

John lulled through Saturdays reading and tinkering with a tape recorder; he hiked with the Boy Scouts and spun the fantasies of a white prince. Ironically, he had a more fortunate upbringing than another alumnus of Hillhouse High School—a white man—who later became mayor. Richard Lee was raised in a cold-water flat by a working-class Irish Catholic family. Graduation from Hillhouse was as far as the Lee family's purse allowed his education to go. Lee worked his way through childhood Horatio Alger style. After five years as a reporter for New Haven's morning paper, he ran successfully for alderman at the age of twenty-three. In 1966, twenty-seven years later, Richard Lee was at the helm of New Haven for the seventh time around and perhaps the fairest-haired mayor in the national spotlight. That was the same year John Huggins packed to go off to college in Pennsylvania. He never reached the age of twenty-three.

But on the surface John Huggins apparently wanted for nothing. Except for a car. If he had a car, he could roll out of New Haven and see what the world was about.

"I'm thinking of heading out to California, to UCLA," came the call to his father in 1966 from Lincoln University. John, now a Navy veteran, was a restless freshman there. "I've got to do something for my people," he explained.

"They're not *your* people!" The father's voice thickened

then, as it does today, with scorn for what he calls the Negro downtrodden. "I know a lot of them, laying about with their hands out, and they're no damn good." New Haven was where John belonged, the father insisted, where his influential white friends could offer opportunities.

But John had seen something of the world by then. He had learned how to kill and how to stay alive as a Class-A radarman in Vietnam. Discharged with a Navy unit commendation, he had returned to enter Lincoln. A near drive from this quiet black college in Pennsylvania John met a high-spirited super-black girl. Her name was Ericka; she was a tall, angry, insistent girl whose militant ideas were new to John. Ericka was not about to stick around West Chester, Pennsylvania, at the proper black Cheyney School, studying to be an old-biddy schoolteacher with the rest of the Oreos.

There was no way for John to explain these things to John Huggins, Sr., permittee of the Fence Club. He and Ericka wanted to get married and get out. So he switched tactics.

"I want to marry a college girl. We'll come home together this summer so you can meet her." The one thing he could really use, John mentioned to his father, was a car.

He got a Plymouth. Mr. Huggins bought it in the fall of 1967 for the couple to drive back to Lincoln University. But they sailed right on by to Southern California, and that was the last time the Hugginses saw their son alive.

Southern California was the ideal tinderbox for Panthermania. Watts offered itself as a reference on one side, and on the other, winding hot off the desert and over the Santa Ana hills, blew a wind that dries out the nerves. If one is looking for them, one can find people as capricious and primitive as that wind, which has a habit of fanning sparks over parched canyons and generating fires that drive men and animals to the sea.

It was all there waiting in and around UCLA. Exotics, parolees, other misfits from retarded hamlets like New Haven, all looking for action with a new, mixed force of black and white revolutionaries . . . known as the Black Panthers. Inevitable. John Huggins was baptized into instant black consciousness.

A ready-made feud existed with the prevailing black nationalist group called US, led by UCLA graduate Ron Karenga, a black separatist who had style and big political ambitions. The Panther movement welcomed white radical support; US stood for black separatism. Karenga and the US organization controlled the federal funds that were coming to Watts from HEW and other sources. But support for the Panthers had begun to build in the Watts community. This put the two organizations at loggerheads, especially since the Panthers had the sympathy of nearly all the blacks at UCLA. Karenga had a string of warriors with Swahili names who were preparing to launch deadly power games on the infant Panther movement.

John and Ericka looked UCLA over as a base for political organizing. Its High Potential program looked fertile, with a black component of fifty scholarship students. They met with Alprentice ("Bunchy") Carter, who agreed. Bunchy was on parole from an armed-robbery sentence and knew the militant black network of Southern California, including a fiery-tongued sister by the name of Elaine Brown. They all joined the High Potential program. Between perfunctory appearances in class they made friends for the cause. Bunchy and John became the brains of the Panther movement in Southern California—Bunchy the number-one man and John the best-liked militant on campus.

"There's real bad blood between the Panthers and US," Bunchy Carter warned the director of the High Potential program. It was the fall of 1968 and John and Bunchy, nearly bounced the previous year for poor academic attendance, were beginning to see certain advantages to getting an education while they were politicizing UCLA. The director was afraid of a war between the rival groups over the selection of a leader for the new Black Studies program.

"If I have anything to do with it," Bunchy assured her, "there won't be any fighting at UCLA."

But the Simba Wachuka (Young Lions), Karenga's goon squad of eighteen-year-olds trained in soul sessions to fight Swahili style, kept elbowing into meetings of the Black Student Union. "We've got a man to head your Black Studies program," ran the Karenga line. "You're politically naïve. Let us run the show and everything will be cool."

The students balked. Finally the Panthers found their political legs in the power vacuum and formed a resistance movement. John Huggins was named chairman of the criteria committee to select a Black Studies program director. But the word was out: "The Simbas are tough. Karenga speaks and they jump."

In January of 1969 Karenga made a personal appearance at a UCLA meeting, accompanied by a full complement of his warriors. With his shaved skull, he was a menacing figure.

"Oppressors come in all colors!" the riled students shouted at him, refusing to be intimidated. Elaine Brown and Bunchy Carter were particularly vocal. Seething in shameful retreat, Karenga made a point of stopping Bunchy Carter. "What do you and the Panthers have to say about all this?" he demanded. Bunchy threw down the gauntlet.

"Power to the students!"

Guns came back with Karenga's goons a week later. Donald Hawkins, a lieutenant from US, collared an unaffiliated black girl on her way out of the final meeting of John Huggins' committee.

"Get to a pay phone, sister. Upstairs by the cafeteria. You put in a call to Jimeni Jomo every fifteen minutes. Tell him Stodi told you to call. Every fifteen minutes, if things are cool, you say into the phone, 'Everything okay,' see? If and when something comes down, you yell *'Vita!'* "

The girl did as she was told because she believed the name Jimeni Jomo belonged to a minor warlord in US.

A getaway car was already backing into a restricted parking lot two hundred yards from the student center. Harry Carey, a UCLA black, spotted them first: Chocheci (Claude Hubert) and Watani (Larry Steiner) and Tuwala (Harold Jones). Three sets of mountainous shoulders draped in dashikis were bulking out of the car doors. The first two men walked nice and loose from the humanities building toward the student center, caressing the guns in their belts. Tuwala went straight for the infamously loud Panther sister Elaine Brown. She happened to be passing alone through the basement of the student center. She was caught unaware, in a black leather coat.

Tuwala hoisted her up by the coat buttons. One ripped off. She gave no scream. This Elaine Brown—who today commands the whole Southern California Panther district—was no helpless hysteric. Her specialty at political meetings was the Pussy Power speech. With it Elaine Brown originated the concept that a woman's function is to use her body to entice men into the Panther party. With the threats of Tuwala, therefore, Elaine Brown dealt one-to-one.

"Get your motherfucking hands off me, nigger!"

Bunchy Carter passed the door just as Tuwala was dropping his hands. Outraged that he had not been summoned, using the white southern vernacular adopted for insults among rival black militants, Bunchy hollered at Elaine, "If a nigger ever grabs you like that again, I want you to hit that nigger!"

John Huggins, ignorant of the developing showdown, was upstairs waiting outside the cafeteria to begin a meeting with black faculty. Bunchy Carter rushed up to report to John. But even as the two Panthers stepped into the cafeteria, Tuwala was already planted front and center on a chair. Facing the door, big as a bull's-eye, Tuwala was ready for all comers.

Just before noon the tip-off girl put in her last call to say "Everything okay." Then gunfire began to screech in the air, ricocheting off walls and thundering out the cafeteria door in volleys of incessant satanic fury. The tip-off girl split. In Swahili, she remembered, *vita* means "war."

John Huggins caught the first dumdum bullet in a vital blood vessel, one-eighth of an inch from his heart. It severed his aorta. John went down for dead. Terrified students pasted themselves on the floor. Now shots began flying from all sides and US goons were coming off the wall, but Bunchy Carter spotted the triumphant way Chocheci held his .38. And then—*tip-tick*—Chocheci slipped a new homemade dumdum bullet into his weapon.

Bunchy leaped over Tuwala's chair with his arms out for the assassin of John Huggins. Chocheci, with a purer aim this time, drove his second bullet into Bunchy Carter's heart. Tuwala split. Steiner was bailing out the second-floor window. But it was not over. With one deafening blast after another, something like cannon fire was bombarding the exit.

John Huggins! His finger was pulling in spasms on the trigger of a .357 Magnum, a weapon powerful enough to make paper clips of a car engine, so deadly that most law-enforcement officers are forbidden to use it. The Magnum seemed to have control of a dead man's hand. John Huggins, sprawled in a lake of backed-up aortic blood with zero elevation, kept hugging the trigger of his Magnum until the Simbas reached their getaway car and roared out of UCLA like a scalded dog. Then the spasms stopped. John Huggins rested on the floor with Bunchy Carter and was quiet.

Reverberations from that brutal shoot-out have not yet stopped. In the first wave all Panther students left UCLA. Bright young black men like John Huggins' best friend, Albert Armor, the son of a Los Angeles doctor, turned bitter; today he is under prosecution for two felony charges. Elaine Brown devoted her life to the Panthers; she now travels the international circuit from Hanoi to Algiers organizing with Third World peoples. But the first order of business was revenge on US. Four Panthers including Elaine Brown turned up to testify at the trial of Karenga's black nationalists.

"We couldn't have prosecuted that case without the Panthers' help," admits an assistant to the Los Angeles district attorney. Three of five men charged with the killings were convicted. Larry Steiner (Watani) and his brother, George Steiner (Sultani Ali), received life sentences. Donald Hawkins (Stodi) was sent to a state prison for youthful offenders. Hubert (Chocheci) and Jones (Tuwala) are still at large.

"The real tragedy of the whole thing was John and Bunchy," says the assistant district attorney. "They and the Panthers were just becoming part of the educational scene at UCLA. They didn't get much of a chance."

As things stood at the end of 1970, according to the Los Angeles district attorney's office, "The names US and Karenga are mud at UCLA. People trying to leave the organization get their apartments firebombed. Ron Karenga and three of his warriors were recently indicted by a county grand jury for torturing two members of US. He is out on bail pending trial. The Panthers in Southern California are now a pretty small group of leftovers. Mostly misfits—angry, unhappy, low-IQ kids. It's sad."

John Huggins became a revolutionary martyr. His bravura death sent shock waves across three thousand miles into the torpid cellars of obediently middle-class young black men with a lust for the apocalypse. Young men like Mentor Jones.

3

FIFTEEN AND BLACK in New Haven, Connecticut . . . unable to be a Panther, unable to sleep—Mentor Jones is the beginning of something else. He knows the John Huggins saga by heart. New Haven, too, is wiser now. The time is May 1970. Panthermania is at its peak. A Black Panther rally has recently gripped the town, and Yale University is still gasping for life. We have come out to Mentor's house because he symbolizes what will happen next in the struggle for black manhood in New Haven.

On the ride out Dixwell Avenue to see Mentor, we made three stops which pretty well laid out where the lines are drawn in a northern black community.

In the American Oil service station we met a friendly young black mechanic. He explained his town in one memorable stroke of doublethink. "In New Haven we're like peas in a pod. The Man does his things on his side of the track, we do ours on our side. *But one thing we don't have in New Haven is segregation.*"

The hippest dudes hang out on the sidewalk where Liggett's wraps around a central corner on Dixwell. A tall, handsome sharpie waved the Panther newspaper at us. He had on this terrific elephant-brimmed Al Capone hat, tilted at a rakish diagonal and bound with an orange bandanna. He kept tapping the hat and smiling and jiving on the corner as if money were suddenly free. It was infectious. We smiled back. He bounded over to sell us a paper and gave us the black-power fist. Then he tilted his hat still further and smiled. We asked him about the hat because it seemed to matter more to him than anything in the paper.

"Dig it," he said. "That's a New Yawk racketeer hat!"

Out past the Eli Clothing Store, on the other side of town from North Haven, where the Polish Falcons gather in Nest 81 and the Broadway service station flies the sign USED BICYCLES—GUNS—MOWERS—BOUGHT AND SOLD, we began driving slowly. We pulled alongside a group of black women in three-button Sunday spring coats. It was a broken-stoop neighborhood near Mentor Jones' house.

"Can you tell us where to turn for Munson Street?" David Parks asked.

"Munson Street? Don't know it. *Mun*son Street?" puzzled the women in birdlike voices. "Jes' keep straight on is best."

The street turned out to be a block away.

When William Jones' two children were born the family lived "on the limb" down in Congoland—that is to say, on Congress Avenue, where the rats run all night inside the walls. His wife worked as a psychiatric nurse, trained at

Bellevue in New York. To get out of Congoland William Jones worked four jobs at once. Before dawn he left to make seat covers for the Avco factory and at night he ran a dry-cleaning business and on the side he sold baby furniture and on the weekends he buttoned up in the white jacket of a steward. Playing the distinguished but mute colored gentleman, William circulated past the elbows of Yale dons until his full beard turned silver. Finally he had one thousand dollars for the down payment on this house. By the time he had it paid for, however, his wife was dead of cancer.

Today William's beard is clipped and juts forward, rather like a Pharaoh's. He is proud of his home in Hamden, a block or so over the New Haven city line, which qualifies as suburban. Things are moving that way now, out Dixwell Avenue from Congoland into a black suburban settlement in Hamden. William put the Volkswagen in the driveway and planted tulips beneath the Japanese maple and this year he put his fifteen-year-old son Mentor in a fancy prep school. Above all he is proud, though uncertain, of his son.

Tip-tick. Tip-tick. Tip-tick. Tip-tick. From the cellar of the Jones house only one sound, small and fitful, has been firing with steady precision for the past hour. Mentor is down in the cellar bunched up and sweating inside his bleached jeans on a secondhand sofa bed and the safe sounds have stopped. The monster flick on TV is off. The air is emptied of anesthesia from the Funkedélics and the inner-ear orgasm of Jimi Hendrix. Mentor has turned them all off. *Tip-tick. Tip-tick.* I have heard this sound before—where?

The cliché thought would be a gun. Assumption: young

and frustrated black boy in a cellar is cocking and firing an unloaded gun. But Mentor is cerebral. This is a controlled, cerebral sound. He keeps the world off balance through the artful use of paradox, such as attending prep school in white Methodist Massachusetts and appearing there as "Daddy" in Albee's *An American Dream.* He also keeps a blue ring-binder notebook. Its cover is decorated with the loves and hates and heroes Mentor carries everywhere with him. *Che. Giap. Commie Crusade. Sarah Weisman* [a prep-school classmate] *not radical but she tries.*

Off	*Viva Libra!*	*Katy—*
the		
Pig!	*Nationalist Red China*	*Lewis Academy*

Inside the notebook is his first play, called *Panther!* Two winters ago he showed it to a young woman, Ericka Huggins, who knew some people in a black community theater group. She said it was good. She was going to run it over to the group's director at Yale Drama School. When Mentor came home from boarding school again, Ericka Huggins was Docket Number 15681 in Niantic Correctional Institution for Women.

She and Bobby Seale and six others are being tried by the State of Connecticut for conspiring to murder Alex Rackley, a suspected party informer. Mentor has had no time for adolescence. He is growing up with a Panther trial in his town.

What is this *tip-tick* sound—this sound of Mentor Jones which singes the air and ticks up the cellarway, building into apprehension? It strains in my ear through some distant consciousness, like a child's stutter.

Upstairs with Mentor's father we are drinking a little Piña Colada before dinner. William Jones apologizes for the bread lumps in his homemade meat loaf. He is a widower. The fierce beauty of his face has lapsed somewhat under the wadding of cheeks and mellowed perspectives of middle age. His muscular frame speaks of raw, uninterrupted physical exertion. Today, though, William's neck is a bit ropy. His midsection has grown pillowy, and the reason he stays home drinking Piña Colada late of a Sunday afternoon is to avoid being trapped by the lusty widow across the street. William's eyes, however, are working eyes. Normally level and amused, when presented with foggy concepts these eyes snap on like high beams. Behind them is a half century of living, ten years of watching black movements rise and fall in New Haven.

CORE, SNCC, the Muslims, now the Panthers . . . William Jones has marked them all. Their discarded leaders remain his friends. About white New Haven he knows what he knows from working weekends as a steward in Yale's private dining clubs. He served the provost and the law-school dean, for instance, while they fretted over the formation of Yale's Black Students Alliance.

"I'd be stupid," William chuckles at his own put-on, "but I was always listenin'."

"Were your kids ever attacked by police in the neighborhood when they were small?" William is asked.

"In *this* neighborhood? This happens to be a jive-ass af-*flu*-ent neighborhood," William says. "We call it Peyton Place."

Everyone laughs comfortably. Upstairs here the air is secure with cooking spinach. We can eat and drink and rationally discuss with Mentor's father the knot in his boy's mind —his obsession with the Panthers. But down in the cellar Mentor is suffering from it. I think about the first time I heard Mentor's voice, a couple of weeks before.

"There's another assassination . . . got to check it out with the party . . . might be this weekend," said the taut voice over a long-distance wire. Mentor's father, whom we'd met while he was acting as a marshal at the May Day Panther rally in New Haven, put us in touch on the upstairs phone.

What assassination? I asked. Who?

"It's in the book, I'll bring you one from the bookstore . . . the Little Red Book," the voice said to me, a total stranger.

What is in the book? "Rules . . . it's a party . . . a party has no room for individual convictions." I froze at that point. Once more the scared voice from a pay phone in Massachusetts reached blindly out, punctuated with gasps of the absurd. "If you don't go along with the assassination, you might be next on the list," it said. When I met Mentor Jones at home in New Haven, he remembered nothing of the conversation.

Stoned and scared at the time? Perhaps, or he might have been putting on a front. Discussing it later face-to-face, Mentor looked suddenly, undeniably fifteen. His solemn face dipped and brooded behind thick glasses. He seemed caught between the narrow chest and crudely bolted limbs of adolescence and a leaping, precocious mind. Sensing his exposure, Mentor said at last of our phone conversation, "I was probably referring to Richard Nixon. He ought to be assassinated."

Panther Chief of Staff David Hilliard was once arrested for making a similar statement. This was another warning that talk is the most unreliable and overreacted-to weapon in the black revolutionary toolbox.

Shortly after New Year's in 1970, Mentor fled prep school in white Methodist Massachusetts and bused home to Hamden. He had decided to join the party. On a night cold enough to crack sidewalks, Mentor announced he was going down to the Panther Defense Committee office to begin his apprenticeship. William said he could stay home and be a Panther.

"The party requires six months on probation," Mentor corrected him. "They investigate. You're either a Panther in good standing or you're not a Panther. You can't just *call* yourself a Black Panther."

Down on Chapel Street in New Haven they would give him a stack of Panther newspapers and he would come back to Hamden to sell them. William said he would probably be shot. If not by a cop, by a neighbor. Hamden's black neighborhood is red-shingle suburban, two-family lawns, little girls with parts between their braids and young dudes in kelly-green trousers. Hamden is alarm clocks going off at five in the morning. Parents who rise to those alarms for jobs in the Winchester gun factory or the Hostess cupcake plant do not take kindly to a teen-age native son out late on the street peddling revolution.

Mentor stood the street-corner test until midnight. He was scared and cold. He sold one paper—to his father. At midnight Mentor headed downtown to Number Nine, the storefront drug-rehab center run loosely by school dropouts in the absence of any other mental-health outlet for New Haveners under sixteen. Kids drop by there not so much to rap about dope as to talk out the knots in their minds. But they were mostly middle-class white kids, Mentor discovered. So again he felt alone and went home.

The next day a friend asked Mentor if he was in. No, Mentor said, he was not in. Membership in the Black Panther Party was closed. Frozen, to protect against police infiltration and power-hungry black political rivals. It was frozen nationally, he found out, when John Huggins and Bunchy Carter were killed at UCLA in January of 1969.

That was over a year ago, Mentor told his friend. "Over a jive-ass year ago!"

Now in Mentor's house, his father looks toward the cellar-way and shakes his head. The boy is probably down there, his father says, running through his mind a picture of John Huggins and his .357 Magnum on the cafeteria floor at UCLA. . . .

. . . *John with a ragged dumdum hole through his chest, drowning in the blood swamp coming up in his mouth, still able to lift a gun out of his belt by sheer force of training in self-defense. Able to squeeze that trigger again and again in postmortem spasms. This was no whimper-tongued white-shoe Yalie copout. This was really it! A half-dead black man and his weapon united in a choreography so exquisite, so instinctual, that the two blasted on beyond death.*

We drink a little more Piña Colada with William and shift uneasily in our chairs. David Parks asks him if Mentor has his notebook downstairs.

"Mentor always has his notebook with him. He says it's his only key to reality."

What strikes home is that today it is natural to think about a very bright and bothered adolescent boy in terms of shooting. The words that pertain are *homicide, suicide, genocide.* At one time these words had highly specific meanings. They have been beaten up in courtrooms and whipped around in the over- and underground press until even these words have become murky, homogenized. We find ourselves in a country which can no longer accurately distinguish between who is doing the killing, being killed or killing himself.

And so we sit inside William's red shingle house, careful to speak in the conditional, and we pretend not to wonder what Mentor is clicking downstairs. His father listens. The worry he does not display.

"How would you feel if one of your friends, say, had a son who was in the Panther party? Say he was given the order to assassinate someone?"

William pushes back from the dinner table. "Well, I don't believe in murder under any circumstances. But I know—I can't say I know, but I can see—that the feelin' of the average member of the Black Panther Party is that they're at war. And they're executin' themselves in the same way as if they were in battle in Vietnam. Some of the fellas are veterans of the Vietnam war. They been taught to kill. They came back, conditions weren't what they expected and they feel that they're at war. Right here."

Out of habit, William goes to the window to check the street. He turns with a protective afterthought. "This is *their* thinkin'. I'm not sayin' it's absolutely *my* thinkin'. But I can kinda pass on their feelin'."

Middle-class black parents are in the same spot as the white liberal parent who wakes up to find a potential bomber in his child's bed. It is the reactions that are different. The fears and agonies of the black parent must be kept private because the fear of white retaliation is greater. Sometimes mixed with vague hopes but more often with convictions born of experience that the price is too high, the torn loyalties of sisters, brothers and friends of black revolutionaries are not made public. They are no less vehement. It is just that the white majority, hearing little about them, generally assumes these feelings don't exist.

William, who would not think of invading his son's sanctuary, excuses himself to get something upstairs. "Don't want you to think I'm passive," he says. With good humor William has shown us his home and tulips and his dead wife's oil paintings, but now he returns with a resolute bearing. Laid flat in his palm is a .38-caliber pistol.

"Do you have that on you all the time?"

"Yes. I wouldn't provoke anything. I'd never use it with troopers around. But if I felt I'd been taken advantage of . . ." William hesitates. "You can't feel safe here these days. If I had to use it, I would."

Tip-tick, tip-tick. It is a rather wimpy sound after all, coming from Mentor. This is no giant phallic blast of gunfire. These are small, steady, cerebral shots, marking time to the knots Mentor is untying in his mind. But one is easily fooled by Mentor, as Mentor himself has been fooled all his life.

They told me I was stupid in first grade. Okay, I'm stupid, so I won't do anything. I didn't know about race and racism. Most of the kids at grammar school were white. One day in front of the class my first-grade teacher said, "I don't like your tie because it's black." I said, "I don't like you." He said, "I don't like you or the color of your tie." Then all the kids repeated after the teacher, "We don't like black." So I came to believe when I was six years old that black was an ugly color.

The fourth grade was the first time I did any work. I went home one day with my friend, name was Timothy. He called me "nigger." That was the first I knew there was any distinction between black and white. "Okay," I said, "so what?"

They put me into the stupid class to learn reading. Then I began to see the racial discrimination in school, the caste system of tracking and channeling. The way I knew was that the smartest kid in the class was white and had blue eyes and blond hair. I think she was stupid. But the ones put into the stupid groups were black children and white working-class students—automatically assumed to be stupid. If one of the other kind was put in a remedial group, the mother would be down at school the next day yelling, "Why is my kid in a stupid class?"

I knew I had some high potential. Based on my first Otis test in grade school, they gave me an IQ of 96.

I was retested later and came out with an IQ of 110.

Now at prep school they tell me I'm exceptional.

They keep changing the answers on Mentor. These days he is taking care to use his bright smile as little as possible.

He prefers to look down and then abruptly up with burning eyes—which takes his listener through the Shift. This is the point known to youngsters when one shifts from being Negro to being black. The Shift is a gear-grinder. Every day the gears slip a little, and while Mentor is fighting to regain control he hides behind a crazy act.

This year the prep-school psychiatrist went into Mentor's head and came out with the neatly printed report that lies on the coffee table:

> Mentor is an exceptional student, though he tested only adequately the first time. He will probably remain at average level with his peers through prep school and only emerge thereafter. Now he has developed the defense of "acting crazy." He is not crazy at all but is down on himself and searching for figures to believe in. Mentor has a history of throwing himself into things 100 percent. Intense, able to deal with complicated abstract thoughts, he then slips into confusion. His artistic outlet is very important. *The most helpful thing for Mentor would be if he could find one adult figure at prep school with whom he could identify.*

"My son and I was talking yesterday about John Huggins," William mentions, "and why he got killed. The way Mentor was runnin' it down to me, there's two factions. The reactionary black nationalists, who want a separate colony and don't believe in organizing with the white revolutionaries. And the Panthers, who do. Well now, the black nationalists are killing all these Panthers, like John Huggins, and gettin' away with murder—"

"Black nationalists are nothing but mirrors of the materialist white society!" The shouted comment comes from the cellarway. So we all take the cue to go downstairs and check what Mentor is doing. He is curled around the blue note-book, his "only key to reality," and writing the manifesto for a new revolutionary party.

Student Organizing of Private Schools:

Teams of politically literate students
must be sent to organize other schools
and aid on drugs, draft counseling,
abortions and other relevant subjects.

(1) Hold student workshops
(2) Free the Student Union
(3) Expose teachers—but do not antagonize them
(4) Be very tacful

Mentor hesitates to show us any more until he has cleaned up the spelling. And worked out his philosophy along more tactical lines—maybe by our next visit.

"Things are moving too fast to waste time talking." He goes back to work on the notebook, tense but absorbed. In his hand is a plastic Paper Mate pen. When he pauses to think against the moving clock how to build a better revolution, he punches the pen point nervously in and out. *Tip-tick.* *Tip-tick.*

Unable to sleep or be a Panther, Mentor Jones last May in New Haven was shooting a ball-point pen. How much time would he have? Before we saw Mentor again, we went back to where Panther fever took hold in New Haven and tried to put some pieces together.

4

January 1969

THE REVOLUTIONARY FUNERAL is a prime recruiting event. When John Huggins came home from college in a coffin, accompanied by his vengeful wife Ericka and their daughter, a whisper of a thing less than a month old, the spark of Panthermania was set off in New Haven. His body arrived by train on January 23, 1969.

"John Huggins? Killed in a militant-type action in California?" whistled his childhood friend, picking up the newspaper outside Yale Medical School. "I knew John was naïve, but I would have pictured him as *last* in line to fight with militant tactics." As the shock subsided, a much crueler question wedged into Walt Johnson's mind. He has not been able to get it out since. *Why did John go through the Shift and I didn't? What put him in a box and me in medical school?*

"If John had come home alive as a Panther, he probably would have told me I couldn't relate to poor black people,"

35

Walt Johnson said, wrestling with the irony. "And here I am, a kid whose father left us on welfare when I was eleven. This is the terrible problem in the black community today, little groups all over the country telling each other, 'Look, we can't relate to you because you're black bourgeoisie now.' Urban games," he finally scoffed. But it was not hard to tell that self-doubt had taken hold of Walt Johnson's mind.

A well-heeled white activist got on the phone to explain John's death to her out-of-town friends. "The shocking thing is that the Huggins family is so clearly social class Number One black," she reported. "They won't talk to anyone about it. The whole thing, from John's marriage to Ericka to John's death, they see as an unmitigated disaster."

From the moment Ericka hit town, little tremors fanned out and quickly grew into frightened rumors. *Had Ericka brought any of those crazy California Panthers back to Connecticut?*

Local people dialed the white activist, knowing she would have an ear to the grapevine. "Ericka was described to me quite frankly by a young black community leader," the activist woman began, speaking confidentially, "as a black Ilse Koch"—letting this penetrate— "*Koshh,* you know, the heartless Nazi sympathizer. The black community here is terrorized by the Panthers. And frankly, I am told by many young militant black men here that the Panther women are uncontrollably aggressive. Man-haters. They take it out through the Panther movement, you see."

"Ericka Huggins? Let's put it this way," said an influential white attorney. "If you invite Ericka to a party she'll bring the boards and you supply the nails. A born martyr."

An appreciative black Yalie, though highly skeptical of the Panthers, looked at Ericka differently. "We've had Erickas all our life. If it weren't for the toughness of black women, we black men would all be like buffaloes. Extinct."

The Hugginses, despite their private bitterness toward Panther ideology, did not have John's hair cut or put him in a gray Episcopalian suit. They bought him a black leather jacket and a beret. Bridgeport had the only Panther chapter in Connecticut at the time; black-booted girls and men in leather body jackets began to turn up at the funeral parlor. By the time big-shot Panthers came from Oakland and Los Angeles, John Huggins was laid out for a full-dress Panther burial.

Two hundred people attended his wake, only a third of them white. Warren Kimbro, soon to become a captain of New Haven's first Panther chapter, read an excerpt from Eldridge Cleaver—the oddly comforting description of a clash in 1967 between Panthers and the Oakland police.

"It was very black, very sad," recalls Fred Harris, who was the strongest black militant in town up to the day of John Huggins' wake. Born with a political folksiness in his fingertips, Freddy was the first local spokesman to make blackness count for something in City Hall when he created the Hill Parents Association back in 1963.

Shortly before John Huggins split for California, he had joined HPA. But as the Hugginses saw it, he became disillusioned with the pacifier relationship between the mayor's office and Fred Harris' organization.

The way Fred Harris tells it, "John always sort of rebelled.

Our parents went to the same church on Dixwell. But the thing is, John used to cut Sunday school to come talk to my group in this shoeshine parlor I ran. He seemed to be a bright little kid."

As Fred Harris spoke, his words grew soft with paternal feeling; his strong sense of bereavement was personal, as though there had been a death in the family: "John was together before he left for Berkeley [*sic*] . . . when he was still working with me in HPA."

While the Huggins funeral caught the imagination of young black New Haven like nothing before or since, it made Fred Harris feel old. He could see his leadership, his Hill Parents Association, indeed his whole era of nonviolent protest, passing overnight into ridicule.

Early February

Showdown between Ericka and the Hugginses. The elderly couple had fulfilled their obligation by giving John a Panther funeral. Now they wanted Ericka to do right by his baby—their grandchild, a tiny precious chip off their son and fragile with three weeks of life. Her name was Mai.

"We've got room for you and Mai and you won't have to buy food or anything."

But Ericka insisted on her own apartment. Then why didn't she leave New Haven and forget the Panthers and raise John's baby safe! they demanded. The Hugginses baptized Mai but lost the showdown. Baby and mother vanished into downtown New Haven.

Ericka Huggins and Warren Kimbro? Their names were linked on the rumor pump, though the connection was unclear. Kimbro was a thirty-four-year-old community youth counselor and the father of two. Was the attraction political or personal?

Rumors of the connection reached Betty Kimbro Osborne, Warren's older sister. She was suspicious of Ericka from the start and made no secret of it. A clash between the two women was inevitable.

Ericka was taller than John Huggins. Of all her imposing characteristics, Ericka's tallness was paramount. Rising five feet eleven inches, slender and firm inside her denim work suit, an energetic twenty-two, she strode around town with her legs cutting like the flash of scissors—and was very soon unmistakable.

This is Ericka Huggins, Connecticut Panther Party Minister of Political Education, is how she announced herself. Not always fiercely, sometimes with the disarming breathlessness of a little girl. She had a little-girl face, oval, with large, dramatic eyes. Her hair was brushed from a center part into two broad wings which further framed her eyes in innocence. Her lips were capable of falling into petulance or delivering a withering scowl. But when the occasion called for softness, Ericka's face melted into the most engagingly girlish smile. She could preside over meetings with the composure of a Rose Bowl queen.

She hailed originally from Washington, D.C. New Haven had never seen anything like her. People wanted to mourn for John Huggins' brave widow. Ericka Huggins wanted to wake them up.

Betty Kimbro Osborne is no less beautiful or fearless than Ericka, but older. Forty, tense, a feet-on-the-ground realist.

She is in the black middle as a Yale faculty wife and not about to apologize. From a family of eight, with all her sisters living unremarkably in Ansonia, Derby, New Haven, and one brother on the Miami police force, Betty Kimbro Osborne alone married *up*.

Ernest Osborne is director of community affairs for Yale. Name any project working between New Haven's town and gown segments and Ernest Osborne's name is on it—though probably in fine print. Modest and principled, reflective behind his horn rims, Ernest Osborne has the quiet man's touch. His name is respected in all circles. In fact, Ernest Osborne is one of the best hopes New Haven has in the wings for a black mayor. Or was.

Ericka avoided confronting Mrs. Osborne on her own turf. Too alien. Together Betty and Ernie Osborne answer the door of their olde Connecticut colonial in matching dashikis, designed by Betty. It is a mixed block with black children and white fuzz and backyard barbecues. Somehow the Osbornes and their two enthusiastic teen-age children seem more New York than New Haven. (Ernie attended Benjamin Franklin High School and Long Island University.) The house is heavy on imports from East Fifty-seventh Street in Manhattan. Design Research pillows and Mexican prints and Scandinavian serving bowls culled from frequent conference trips. Form is important to Betty Osborne. But so are people. She has worked seven years for New Haven's Redevelopment Agency. (What the Panthers would call "a house-folk gig.") She also belongs to Black Women for Progress.

One would not like to be the enemy of either of these

women. Betty Osborne combines the high carriage of an *Essence* model and the tenacity of a Jewish mother. Ericka Huggins is taller and at that time had less to protect.

Ericka finally confronted Betty by phone. "I hear you and Black Women for Progress want to whip my ass and run me out of town."

"Who gave you that piece of information?"

"Never mind who. Your organization doesn't want people coming in from out of town and breaking up other people's homes, right? The fact is I'm here to help people."

"If you won't give me your sources, don't call me up with that dumb shit," said Betty Kimbro Osborne. "In the first place, I think you should leave town and raise your daughter. In the second place, when and if I get ready to go after your ass I won't need any women's group to do it."

Mid-February

Their faces broke into Channel 8 news during the dinner hour. Ericka Huggins and Warren Kimbro, along with a Bridgeport Panther by the name of Jose Gonzales. Ericka did all the talking. Right on, brother! New Haven was getting together a brand-new Black Panther Party chapter.

Warren Kimbro stopped answering his sister's phone calls. Warren's wife Sylvia wanted to talk to Betty but not on the telephone. One day Sylvia asked if she might send their two children, nine and ten, over from Orchard Street for a few days. The implication was that her husband's political activities and their marriage were not mixing. But the children were never sent to Betty and communications from Orchard Street ceased. Betty began to twitch and jump in her sleep. Her brother's family ties were abruptly suspended—he belonged to something else.

"Don't interfere," Betty's husband counseled. "Warren is almost thirty-five, after all."

"*Someone* has to find out what changes he's looking for that can't take place without his getting involved in the Panther party."

Betty's husband promised to talk to Warren. Betty patrolled through the house tucking in children and making lists from Julia Child's cookbook and came back to bed, more agitated.

"But Uncle is a believer. He's loyal to the extreme. If my brother believes in Mother's Milk, he will give his full support to Mother's Milk. I will never forgive myself if—"

But Ernest Osborne, who had an early meeting with the black faculty, was asleep.

5

WARREN KIMBRO was a good black burgher of New Haven. Until 1969, when he caught Panthermania and killed a man, Warren Kimbro was right down the black middle.

Imagine now—to catch the schizoid pull on Warren Kimbro over the past ten years—that you are standing with one foot in each of New Haven's two hubs.

One foot is on the Green facing Yale. You are in the castle garden encircled by garret tops and gargoyles leaping off the turrets of a great university. Mighty gates curl back benevolently, beckoning—yes, you—into the courtyards of autonomous Oxonian colleges. (But you are dark-skinned and never finished high school.) The people all around you are young and vanilla, with raspberry cheeks and the telltale moles of high breeding. Couples fleet by in tennis whites. Everyone seems limber with life . . . loopy in the ankles from hopping between sailboats and marina docks and from playing the grass and court games common to Nantucket summers.

Late afternoon now. The nation's future elite assembles in

the Karmelcorn Shop to buy ice cream and hash pipes. (You only live in New Haven; Yale *is* New Haven.) Sun settles into the ivy whiskers of libraries and seeps through the leaded glass windows—yes, come: it is time to write sitting-room essays. Everywhere the atmosphere dispenses with the commonplace and carries the assumption of power. It invites the chosen to meditate on where to take the world next time around. You are letting go now to the English tradition . . . entering the province of scholar kings which caused even Warren Kimbro to dream white.

The other foot is in Congoland. In the bathroom of a rooming house. This is one of the shooting galleries along Congress Avenue and you are chipping a little heroin under the skin of your knee. It doesn't show there.

Congoland is a wedge of streets which form the core of New Haven's seven inner-city neighborhoods. It is near Yale. But on each of these corners the brothers of college age, unemployed, stand around in little clots with their young muscles bumping up through short-sleeved shirts and nothing to do but rap. And rap some more, or hustle or sip a little vodka, or shoot. Across the street from the bathroom shooting gallery sags an apartment house, condemned long ago by the Redevelopment Agency. Paste-ups of old Panther newspapers hang off its brick face like dead skin off sunburn. The famous Bobby Seale cover is there. You would recognize it as the drawing made of Chairman Seale being transported from the Chicago conspiracy trial to the New Haven murder trial. Bobby is strapped into an electric chair. His eyes bulge over the headline:

THE FASCISTS HAVE ALREADY DECIDED IN ADVANCE
TO MURDER CHAIRMAN BOBBY SEALE
IN THE ELECTRIC CHAIR

But you arc too busy to absorb local color. Police have these shooting galleries staked out. You keep one eye on the exit—this is a constant about being black. It goes for the "distinguished colored gentleman" who serves at Yale club tables as well as the addict. One eye must always be kept on the exit.

Warren Kimbro passed thirty-four years picking his way between these two extremes. For the well-behaved Negro he was right on schedule. He quit high school to follow his brother into the Air Force and came out of the service in 1956—two years after the Supreme Court insisted, finally, on integrated schools. But Warren was already twenty-two and running on the old black schedule. Not quite certain what could be done with his life. His assets were small: a handsome face, gentle eyes, evangelical urges and the GI Bill. He was also wiry and tense, but not one to complain aloud. Warren trained as a clothes spotter. That put him in the dry-cleaning business for the next six years. Still on schedule, he switched to making pastries in the Hostess cupcake factory.

"There was no colored, I mean, no black foremen at that time," recalls a black co-worker, Jerry Nelson. "Warren's function was, he was a fruitmaker. Like me. The first community activity Warren got involved in was Residential Youth Center. That wasn't till 1966. But to me, he's always been an extremist." To Jerry Nelson, as to most black New Haveners, "extremist" means anyone willing to act full time on what he believes.

Forty percent of black New Haveners were affected by redevelopment. Some of them began to catch on. Politicians were up to an old trick—using federal renewal programs to finance capital-improvement projects. When envious mayors from other cities came to take notes on the Model City, they were squired past the exciting buildings going up to house merchants, office workers, hotel conventioners and luxury-apartment dwellers. And past the architectural goodies in store for Yale and corporations that had the money to erect monuments to themselves. Housing for the poor was another story—one on which too little reporting came too late.

Not until 1968 did researchers, hired to project the city's needs, discover the 23,500 people who still lived in overcrowded housing and the nearly 4,000 more who lived in substandard housing.

Undaunted, downtown New Haven emerged with its nose powdered. A two-level shopping mall, propped by the new Macy's and the new Park Plaza Hotel, encloses the sounds and smells of modern commerce. The air is washed in cosmetic perfumes and essence of Muzak. The inner windows of Church Street Mall stores are also in a state of perpetual cleansing. Black men with tin pails and rubber squeegees are still wetting, scraping, wiping the Man's windows to help him sell shoes and lipstick.

Inside Macy's the tape-deck voice of modern retailing breaks into the air at exactly 2:04 P.M. *Sales Managers/*

Please take your two-o'clock readings/Take your two-o'clock readings.

Outside, on the sidewalk between the grand old husk of the Taft Hotel and the tall, sanitary, refrigerated Park Plaza Hotel, the little black boys are still lining up with shoeshine kits.

New Haven's new downtown is dedicated to drivers: to docile black families who drive stubby Mercurys and the farmers who roll in from the Valley to shop every Saturday. The fortunes of the city, siphoned off until 1963 by the same suburbanization that undercut other American cities, have indeed improved. Retail sales were up 40 percent by 1968.

The poor people who were scattered in the process of commitment to *things* do not show in the new Church Street complex. Its centerpiece is Paul Rudolph's cathedral for cars. One wonders. When they dig us up, will twentieth-century social history be writ in parking garages?

To appease the finest black families, John Johansen was commissioned to do a brand-new Dixwell Avenue Congregational Church. Something about it—the hidden windows?— makes white people hurry past. A big circular fortress, the church backs off the street into a dust lot. Secretive, defensive. Every window is hidden behind a gusset of concrete. It is as though the architect's hand were guided by news accounts of the future to design a refuge from the urban race war.

Waiting . . . Warren Kimbro kept waiting for an opening in community work. Married to a pretty New Haven girl, father of a son and daughter, he went back to pass the High School Equivalency Test. When the Redevelopment Agency took shape in 1963, he applied to be a housing inspector. High school diploma required. Friends advised Warren to lie about how he got his diploma. Not me, Warren said, these things have a way of catching up with a man. Application denied.

"Citizen participation," the term and the afterthought, did not emerge through the great national dust storm of urban renewal until 1966. Congress passed the Model Cities program and its author, Lyndon Johnson, tied certain people-oriented conditions to the purse strings. The Department of Housing and Urban Development went so far as to issue guidelines for applicant cities on how to ensure "widespread citizen participation."

This must have struck Warren Kimbro funny, and Fred Harris even funnier. Harris had formed his Hill Parents Association three years before—the only real grass-roots group to come forward from the inner city. They had been trying since 1963 just to be recognized by New Haven officialdom.

HPA was small but persistent. It came out of the Hill neighborhood, the largest low-income neighborhood in the central city. All the help-us-first statistics were on the side of the Hill: highest infant-mortality rate, nearly one-quarter of the city's substandard housing, double the city's total unemployment rate. But the city had chosen more malleable neighborhoods to demonstrate its rehabilitative goodwill. New Haven virtually ignored the Hill. Injury was added to insult when the refugees of relocation elsewhere squeezed into the Hill. More strain dragged on the neighborhood's century-old schools, stinking sewer system and one tiny park.

Fred Harris' group never did get the city to honor their proposals for citizen participation. HPA threatened the comfortable bureaucracy set up by Mayor Lee to deal with the poor's problems *for* them. But HPA did clean up its own decaying neighborhood school. In the process, local blacks got their first political education in how to deal with their own problems.

"Fred Harris is a lot like my brother Warren," reflects Betty Osborne. "Freddy is a good, good person, beautiful with children, a gentle man. What burns me up is how everybody uses Freddy. I've seen dudes on the street do it, certainly people in the antipoverty agencies do it. When anybody wants to bring attention to a grievance they call Freddy. They know he's never going to refuse them. But when Freddy's having trouble these same people say, 'Serves him right—that nigger's always messing around here.' "

Warren Kimbro was to have the same painful experience. Being abused by whites is an old story. Being used by blacks was not yet within the realm of imagination.

Passing thirty, Warren Kimbro broke away from the security of making fruit pies. He volunteered as a youth counselor for Community Progress, Inc. (the local OEO office). He loved kids and worked conscientiously. CPI promoted him to community coordinator in his own neighborhood. Things were happening, but slowly. Still on the old black New Haven schedule.

Emotional disturbances tripled in the Hill during 1966.

A little political education is a dangerous thing, especially for black citizens who have nothing to lose but their own ignored, bloated, rotting neighborhood. In the spring of 1967 Fred Harris and others of HPA went to New Haven's progressive "human renewal" agency, CPI, to ask for $37,000. No one wanted a riot. Summer was coming and summers in American cities had become synonymous with riots. HPA wanted the funds to operate three simple programs for the hard-core unemployed. Resistance mobilized. Months of deliberation dragged into the summer. That was the summer when everything began to go backward in New Haven.

The riot erupted—guess where?—in the Hill. Even with Fred Harris and his friends running a valiant peace-keeping operation for the police, New Haven's "disturbance" lasted four days. The Irish and Italian shore towns are still nervous from it. A gun by the bedside goes without saying.

The riot blew the whistle on shocked white liberals. What followed only confirmed what black citizens had suspected: the city responds only to crisis. New Haven's 1967 crisis was the beginning of real fights to make antipoverty funds work for the people, of empty churches being reborn as teen-age soul centers, and of rising expectations that rubbed the nerves raw with waiting.

By 1969 a strong Black Coalition had put itself together. Combining the forces of some forty local groups, it had to be dealt with. Residents of the inner city insisted on manning their own redevelopment offices.

Into this climate of fragile, hard-won hope burst the Panthers.

"With all the dynamics going on in New Haven's black community," explained a Coalition member, "a few people came in to establish a local Panther group. They wanted strong members fast. It started one hell of a fight."

6

March 1969

WARREN KIMBRO FACED his first loyalty test as an apprentice Black Panther.

National headquarters sent word that the Bridgeport chapter had no official Panthers except Jose Gonzales. And even he was under suspicion. "If you see Gonzales, hold him," Warren was ordered—presumably meaning that Kimbro should physically detain him.

Amateurs. As far as Betty Osborne could see, there wasn't a sophisticated revolutionary in the lot. She was comforted, too, by learning that her brother's application to the party would take six months to be approved.

"So much of it is ego and sex." Betty was now trying to comfort her brother's wife, Sylvia. "If Ernie grew a beard and walked out on the Green shouting 'All Power to the People' and 'Motherfucker,' he'd have those suburban housewives following him like the Pied Piper."

Warren's wife, however, cared less and less for the people

hanging around her apartment. She went to Legal Aid. There was talk of a divorce, which brought Betty Osborne back to the boiling point.

She intended to give conciliatory advice. But when she finally got a call through to her brother, the talk quickly disintegrated into the insults born of fear.

"How the hell do you even *know* they're Panthers?" Betty demanded.

"I know."

"Uncle, any dude can put on black leather and come up from Bridgeport with a big line."

Warren said he had been frustrated too long. His life was going nowhere. He wanted to see some real changes in New Haven for a change.

"You're grasping at the first thing to come along!" Betty countered. "Look at all you have to lose—your wife and kids. . . ." Letting this penetrate, "Listen to me! Has the Hag ever given you phony advice?" Warren's pet name for his outspoken sister was the Hag. Now her words were nothing but a trickle in his ears.

Betty laid her trump card on him.

"They'll put you out there to do all kinds of dirt and then you watch, Uncle—they'll pull out on you the minute the shit comes down!"

"Okay, Hag." Warren gave a final, affectionate laugh. "I'll watch my step."

April

Official: Warren Kimbro's apartment at 365 Orchard Street had become Panther headquarters in Connecticut. As a setting it didn't seem to fit. This was no slum basement shared by derelicts and vermin . . . it was not even remotely similar to the old carpenter-Gothic frame houses on the other side of Orchard Street where eccentric roomers sat rocking in dark glasses and baseball caps, waiting to die.

Warren lived in an attached town house. Modern motor-inn style, it was one of the low-middle-income co-ops that drove out the poor during New Haven's romance with the bulldozer. Zinnias in its family gardens. Children playing tag around the outdoor gallery hung over its parking garage. Lots of children.

By now Warren Kimbro was in all the way—his home, his salary, his life and his agonized wife, who decided the lesser of two evils would be to stay there with the children and cope.

At this time, on a national level, Stokely Carmichael broke completely with the Panther party. Tears were few for the former leader of the Student Nonviolent Coordinating Committee. He had been given a top-leadership position in the BPP as a tribute, but not without reluctance on the part of founders Eldridge Cleaver and Huey Newton. There was a major conflict: the Panther party was committed to uniting in the revolutionary struggle with white radicals. Other black-power organizations such as SNCC and US, the West Coast black nationalist faction, were dead set against it; they required strict black separatism. This the Panthers condemned as racist. Months of feuding between Stokely and Eldridge exposed the growing contempt of younger militants for Stokely's attitude. Stokely was ultimately branded a hangover hero with a now irrelevant black nationalist hang-up.

George Sams, a volatile Panther stalwart, was relieved as Stokely's bodyguard. Unlike the others, Sams was very upset by his leader's downfall. But no one paid attention to George Sams until much later in New Haven.

Stokely, maintaining a distant dignity in Guinea, sent his wife to meet the press at Kennedy Airport with a letter in which he warned against the high authoritarianism of the Panthers:

> . . . The present tactics the party is using to coerce everyone to submit to its authority . . . the demand for loyal and unquestioning followers rather than critical colleagues . . . will lead the BPP to become, at worst, a tool of racist imperialists used against the black masses. . . .

Ericka Huggins, meanwhile, was becoming very popular among kids in the Liberation Children's School on Lamberton Street. Children were given breakfast at the Legion Hall and ferried to a former Episcopalian church. A few black and white Yalies taught them in a relaxed atmosphere. Fred Harris' children were among them. They reported home that Ericka was "fantastic."

It was school policy that no political message be forced on the children. They came to school with their parents' politics . . . and, as another teacher said, "The parents weren't *against* the Panthers, but they weren't out selling Panther newspapers either."

May

The Bridgeport Panther chapter folded. Jose Gonzales, the chapter treasurer, dropped out of sight. New York was also in bad trouble, with twenty-one Panthers arrested and charged with complicity in a bomb plot. Every political organization has its regional prejudices. And from the Oakland perspective, these East Coast brothers running around calling themselves Panthers must have looked like a bunch of loud-mouthed, chicken-tailed rubes. The Central Committee wanted a purge. Informers had to be cleaned out.

National officials Landon Williams and Rory Hithe were dispatched from headquarters in Oakland "to straighten out the party on the East Coast." The two officials were bright, militant, dedicated but otherwise quite dissimilar. The contrast in their backgrounds represented the party's effort to unite well-educated blacks with the lumpenproletariat.

Rory Hithe was eighteen, bred in the ghettos of Los Angeles and Oakland. He had spent most of his "adult" life in jail. Landon Williams had left his home town in North Carolina to attend Merritt College in Oakland. Merritt was the junior college attended by Huey Newton. Williams majored in chemistry and passed three years as a student there. At the age of twenty-four he had an honorable discharge from the Army as a paratrooper, a wife and no police record.

Connecticut was the first concern of Hithe and Williams. Ericka warned the New Haven chapter, which was less than four months old, that Central Committee people were coming. She confirmed the official status of George Sams, Rory Hithe and Landon Williams. Williams would be in overall charge.

On May 14, the eve of the purge, Landon Williams made a statement to a meeting of Connecticut revolutionaries, the irony of which struck home only much later.

"There are no Panthers in Connecticut except Ericka," he said.

As far as Warren Kimbro knew, the plan for the weekend was to picket an Adam Clayton Powell rally in Hartford. From then on he would take orders. But one does not have to be a Panther to catch—or be caught for—Panthermania.

7

Saturday, May 17

CONFUSION. MEETINGS. Vague orders being dispatched. Doors slamming at 365 Orchard Street and people leaving for Hartford. The way the front and back doors were flapping and people knocking each other down to get in and out of Warren Kimbro's house, it might have been Stop and Shop.

George Edwards, another aspiring Panther, and Kimbro were the only New Haveners there. Ericka Huggins was the only accredited Connecticut Panther present. Yet through Warren's apartment during that weekend there passed, on faith, more than a dozen near-strangers from other cities.

The action began when Landon Williams and Rory Hithe drove up with George Sams and a square, semiliterate youth named Alex Rackley, an instructor in martial arts from the New York Panther chapter. They had picked him up on the streets of New York, Rackley thought, to provide extra security for the impending visit of Bobby Seale. Rackley presumably figured he was in for the thrill of his life. He was accustomed to sticking out like a minor sore thumb in the New York Panther organization. For once he was running with the big-time dudes.

Dapper Lonnie McLucas checked in with pretty Peggy Hudgins; both were survivors from the Bridgeport chapter. McLucas was twenty-four, with movie-star good looks and quite a volatile history behind him. Originally from Wade, North Carolina, he had been organizing for the Panthers in Delaware and New Jersey before moving on to Bridgeport. Before that he did several years in prison. In 1963 McLucas had been charged with rape, robbery and malicious mischief in Port Chester, New York. He admitted to taking part in the rape of a black woman with another man. But at his trial the young defendant pleaded guilty to a lesser charge and was convicted only of conspiracy to commit robbery. He was given a three-and-a-half- to seven-year sentence on that felony count. Paroled after serving part of his sentence, McLucas disappeared. The handsome wanderer was still wanted in New York on a parole violation when he turned up in New Haven.

Such behavior did not fit at all with Lonnie's appearance. He looked shy, romantic, gentle in the way that draws sighs from mothers. His high forehead smoothed up from widely set eyes, conveying all the innocence of a young boy.

More girls arrived on Orchard Street. Incredible female traffic passed the neighbors' zinnias and baffled stares! Peggy Hudgins, married and the mother of two, was only one of several followers Lonnie McLucas had won while working his way up the East Coast. There was also Peggy's sister, Frances Carter, twenty-one, who had a direct and sensible air about her. She arrived dressed with working-girl chic: bold silver hoops through her ears, the shortest of black leather minis and the slender legs to go with it. Frances worked in a Bridgeport factory, commuting there from her parents' home in Trumbull, Connecticut. In fact, she appeared to be the only one present holding a steady job at the time. But this was Saturday. She was curious. As it turned out later, she also was pregnant.

Following Frances was Loretta Luckes, twenty-two, from Bridgeport. She had applied only twenty-eight days before as an apprentice Panther. Next came the irresistible Rose Marie Smith, with her hair still short and tight to the scalp as a baby's. She was a young-looking sixteen and often lied about her age. All disappeared into the motel-modern interior of Apartment 3-B.

The apparent motivation for being on one's best revolutionary behavior was that Chairman Bobby Seale was arriving Monday to deliver a speech at Yale.

Alex Rackley's exuberance faded slowly. Despite the fact that several hours after his arrival in the paranoid Panther milieu of New Haven Rackley was cast in the role of a suspected informer, the danger did not seem to register with him. Attention was being paid to the minor militant. Perhaps he was preoccupied with the promise of being a star.

"Rackley should be kept overnight," Kimbro and Ericka were told on Saturday afternoon by the visiting Central Committee officers, Landon Williams and Rory Hithe. Their next order was, "Send George Edwards out for hamburgers.

But watch him. He might make a call from the drugstore."

Now, there was a puzzle. Among members of the Yale-affiliated Black Arts Theatre group, all George Edwards was famous for was being a fine actor. Unforgettable in a turban and accompanied by Gregorian chant, he had played the bedeviled George in *Who's Afraid of Virginia Woolf?* Was George Edwards being cast as an understudy for the role of informer?

Sunday, May 18

Two girls barely past puberty strayed in with vacant eyes and cardboard suitcases.

"Lonnie's friends from New Jersey," somebody said.

Ericka and George Sams ordered one child to the kitchen to boil water. The second stray child was ordered to sleep with the suspect Rackley to get information out of him. The air pulsed with crosscurrents of suspicion. George Sams had just put Rackley in the cellar. He was about to direct the interrogation of Rackley and to record the proceedings on tape for national headquarters.

According to party rules, "Individualism on the body is counterrevolutionary." Meaning: individualized sex has no place in party activities. Personal relationships bring with them personal loyalty pulls and "subjective problems." The disciplined revolutionary must be cool of heart and objective of mind. This did not seem to inhibit the romantic Lonnie McLucas nor the exuberant Peggy Hudgins. They had fallen in love at first sight on February 3.

Lonnie was at pains to prove his mettle to Peggy, which under the circumstances would not be easy. Lonnie and the two local brothers, Warren Kimbro and George Edwards, were low men on the totem pole. While the big shots waltzed in and out to Hartford, dropping orders, these three were left home with the girls to mind Rackley.

"Call Trailways bus company," came a surprise directive from Sams to Kimbro. "Find out what it costs to go down to New York." Alone briefly with his charge, Sams considered turning Rackley loose. He offered him three dollars. Rackley complained he couldn't find a jacket. A jacket—what kind of jive excuse was that! Sams ordered the victim taken from the cellar to an upstairs bedroom, where the interrogation resumed in earnest.

George Sams projects the air of a street-corner hipster in early-fifties shoulder pads. There is no mistaking the old diddy-bop walk, that sinking-down-in-the-ankles glide with a break in the knees. At one time it was the only way a black street kid could show he was tough. George was raised poor in the South by his father. Three times shunted into mental institutions, he was labeled at Creedmoor State Hospital in Queens a "dangerous mental defective." On George the Afro, the badge of modern militancy, never quite came off. It looked more like a pompadour.

George has been expelled twice by the Black Panther Party. Or once. It depends on which day one asks.

"It was only once I was put out the party, when I was expelled out by Chairman Bobby Seale," Sams later decided under cross-examination. "But I was reinstated by Stokely Carmichael."

Alex Rackley had claimed he could not read. But on Sunday morning Sams found him lying in bed with *Selected*

Military Writings of Mao Tse-tung. Outrageous! Ericka was called in.

"So then the brother [Rackley] got some discipline in the area of the nose and mouth," said Mrs. Huggins, describing the scene while Sams tape-recorded her voice, "and the brother began to whimper and moan. We began to realize how phony he was and that he was either an extreme fool or a pig. So we began to ask questions with a little coercive force and the answers came after a few buckets of hot water. We found out that he was an informer."

Monday, May 19

Zwiiiiiing!

Just like that into the thick middle-night air a rifle shot smacked wood. Warren Kimbro rushed downstairs. He found a hole through his coffee table. The rifle, brought by Hithe and hidden by Kimbro in the drawer, had shot off by itself through the coffee-table drawer. Off on its own violence trip.

This started Monday off badly.

It was the day of Chairman Seale's speech at Yale. June Hilliard, brother of Panther Chief of Staff David Hilliard, was also scheduled to arrive. Activity on Orchard Street stepped up to a feverish pitch.

Sobbing and choking on the upstairs bed in Apartment 3-B, Alex Rackley pulled out names, and more names: "Steve . . . Janet . . . Jack Bright . . . Abkar . . . Lonnie Epps . . . I heard a conversation between Janet Serno and Inspector Hill of the Twenty-eighth Precinct . . ."

The smell was terrible. Rackley lay in the squalor of his own urine and feces. The young girls sneaked in to swab the victim's boiled skin with a cold cloth. At one point even Sams paused to give his captive a cold shower.

It went like that into afternoon. A scramble-minded boy sang an operetta out of the telephone book, longing to impress his inquisitors, while his indecisive brothers and sisters copied every police interrogation technique they knew (presumably in the interest of their own survival).

After lunch Sams was given orders by Williams and Hithe. "Get Rackley ready to be taken away. Find a car. Call Hartford and tell those dudes to bring down some political power." (On the phone the phrase for guns is "political power.") The officials left and confusion resumed.

Fortunately Williams and Hithe were not around when the Hugginses, John's parents, unexpectedly drove by. The elderly couple had not seen Ericka for more than a week. They were out searching for their granddaughter, Mai.

"We have some baby clothes . . ."

But Ericka had already left Orchard Street.

Alex Rackley began improving. He even fingered New York State Panther Party Chairman David Brothers and his secretary, Rosemary, for telling tales on the New York Panther 21. *Before* the arrest of the Panther 21 for a bomb conspiracy.

"Chairman Brothers and them were saying on the thing—like Alexander's, Macy's and Bloomingdale and Botanical Gardens—that all this added up to the thing that was on the indictment of the twenty-one brothers."

His inquisitors apparently liked the Chairman Brothers

story; people are always delighted by imagining corruption in the highest places. Rackley built on it. He accused Chairman Brothers of being sympathetic to Ron Karenga, the California leader of the US faction that killed John Huggins.

Rackley droned on, barely coherent, until something in this lunatic scene hit Lonnie McLucas as weird.

"Lumumba Shakur," offered the young man on the bed.

"That's no name!" McLucas blurted.

But the game had gone too far and big shots were in town and the locals on Orchard Street presumably needed more to build a purge on than a whimpering, tortured half-wit. Landon Williams returned and criticized the insecure way Rackley was tied. "Use coat hangers." His followers fashioned a wire noose for Rackley's neck.

Hopefully this evidence of businesslike interrogation would impress June Hilliard, who was coming to town with Chairman Seale.

The important people then drove off to Ericka Huggins' apartment, where Bobby Seale was to arrive. Warren Kimbro remembers being told to find another apartment, where Chairman Seale could later speak to all Panthers from Connecticut. In the late afternoon Kimbro met Seale's car at the Oak Street connector downtown and led him to Ericka's apartment. Things grow murkier at this point because nobody wants to remember aloud exactly what Chairman Seale said and did before leaving New Haven the next morning.

Mr. and Mrs. Huggins did stop by Ericka's apartment, still searching for the baby, Mai. Startled by Seale's presence, Mr. Huggins hid the pain behind his face and asked one question:

"What happened to the men who killed my son?"

"They're in jail," answered Seale.

Kimbro then drove June Hilliard, accompanied by Landon Williams and an unidentified man, back to 365 Orchard Street (according to Kimbro's testimony) to see chapter headquarters and to hear the Rackley tapes. The captive's voice was heard rising out of his humiliation in the upstairs bed. "Is Chairman Bobby going to have me killed?"

"I'm not concerned with you," June Hilliard scoffed (according to testimony). "You're a pig."

That evening during Bobby Seale's speech before Yale's Black Ensemble Theatre Company, a little girl belonging to a member of the audience was lost.

"Diane Tomey is missing," Chairman Seale announced. Most of the Panthers went off in search of the missing child. Somehow the Chairman's meeting with Connecticut rank and file never took place.

Warren Kimbro went home from Seale's speaking engagement to count the money donated. He fell asleep after midnight. When Ericka woke him on the morning of May 20, she told him that Chairman Seale had stopped by Orchard Street to use the phone and then left town. They hadn't wanted to wake Kimbro (according to Kimbro's testimony).

George Sams later gave a different account of the previous day's activities. He and Seale, Rory Hithe and Landon Williams all drove back with Kimbro to Orchard Street, Sams insists. When Chairman Seale was presented with Alex Rackley and asked what was to be done with him, Sams recounts this as Seale's answer: "What do you do with a pig? Off him."

By Chairman Seale's own account, he did stop at Kimbro's apartment after his speech to make a phone call. But of the small-potatoes interrogation upstairs he knew nothing. He claims he met George Sams only once, in 1968. Had he known of the brutal scene he would have expelled the guilty members. But according to Seale, the hierarchy of the Panther party can't be expected to have time for policing the rank and file.

"I'm just the chairman," says Seale. "I don't pay attention to everyone."

Tuesday, May 20

Orders had not been carried out. Rackley was not dressed to be taken away. The guns had not arrived from Hartford. George Edwards was conspicuous by his absence. The orders had been: "Get Edwards over here; we can take care of him at the same time." When Landon Williams and Rory Hithe returned to Orchard Street Tuesday morning, all the harassed officials could manage was to reprimand Lonnie McLucas for pulling a blank on help from Hartford. Warren Kimbro never did make the ordered call to Edwards.

New orders started flying. "Put Kimbro on the phone to Hartford. Sams and the girls go up and cut Rackley loose. Get the rifles downstairs. Get dressed in dark clothes. And put your asses in gear!"

A local newspaperman arrived that afternoon to interview the Panthers "about your different programs around New Haven." Chatty . . . a few Panthers giving a living-room interview around a coffee table in which the cantankerous rifle was hidden—while Alex Rackley lay spread-eagled and naked on the upstairs bed, alternately being scalded, bathed and recorded for headquarters.

Hithe returned during the interview; Williams followed after the reporter had gone. About now these two officials sent to straighten out the East Coast reportedly began to lose their grip.

Was this any way to run a political purge? But the voicing of doubts would have been a dangerous, counterrevolutionary act.

The appointed disciples noticed something curious about Rackley as they led their shaky captive out the kitchen door to a waiting car Tuesday night. The coat hanger around his neck stuck out. Kimbro threw a green bush jacket over Rackley's shoulders to hide the hanger. (In the pocket was a phone message taken by Ericka Huggins for Bobby Seale which began: *Don't come to Oregon.* That little clue was discovered later under the dead body.)

According to Sams, but unknown to his two cohorts, Sams had been given orders to kill Kimbro and McLucas if they showed any "nervous tendencies" after helping him dispose of Rackley.

"Power to the People!"

Landon Williams managed that last battle cheer for his bumbling disciples, and shoved a .45 through the car window to George Sams. Sams took out a joint. Kimbro climbed into the front seat and Lonnie McLucas, as was his habit, said, "Right on!"

On the way to his death, young Rackley warned George Sams not to smoke pot while driving. "The police might see you," Rackley said.

At the edge of a Middlefield swamp off Route 147, a boggy no-man's-land near the Powder Hill ski area, Lonnie McLucas stopped the car. He flipped up the hood to suggest engine trouble. With Rackley reluctantly leading, the four men filed into the swamp.

"Got a boat waitin' for you in there," Sams said encouragingly.

The pathetically naïve figure of Alex Rackley stared into blind midnight darkness. He shifted from one foot to the other. The ridiculous costume hastily assembled for him and tied with a rope around his waist hung off his blistered skin. He was barefoot.

"You kin take the boat to New York or Florida or anywhere, but don't you never come back," Sams said, "or Williams'll kill me."

But Rackley was afraid to go barefoot into the swamp. He said he was afraid of snakes.

"Off him," Sams finally said. He laid the .45 in Warren Kimbro's hand and Kimbro walked Rackley a little way into the swamp and put a bullet through his head.

Lonnie McLucas had this crazy unrevolutionary picture running through his mind—the picture of his sweetheart, Peggy Hudgins, crying as he drove off. He had told her they were driving Rackley to the bus station. Now the warm gun returned by Kimbro was placed in Lonnie's hand by Sams and the last order came down.

"Go in there and finish him off."

Lonnie McLucas slogged over the marsh floor until his foot hit a body sprawled in the murk. He left a second bullet in Rackley's chest.

"We may have to make a run for it if trouble arises," Sams warned on the getaway drive. Suddenly the bottom was dropping out of his voice. The lonely and hideous truth of "political assassination"—when left to the lumpen-proletariat who cannot afford the simplest social bonds in their struggle to survive at one another's expense—fell out of George Sams' mouth.

"We're not big shots. We could be killed."

His words put a freeze on the bad air between Sams and his silent accomplices. Then the nervous diddy-bop militant threw six live shells from the .45 out the car window. This enabled Sams to boast back at headquarters: "We shot him eight or nine times."

8

Aftermath

FISHERMEN DISCOVERED RACKLEY the next day on their
way home from work. The call from Connecticut state troopers hit New Haven police headquarters late Wednesday afternoon.

*The body of a dead Negro male has been discovered in a
marshland near Middlefield.*

No great surprise. Police later admitted they knew someone was being held by the Panthers on Orchard Street.

Chief of Police James Ahern immediately met with a
young lady described as a "confidential and reliable informant whom [they] had known for a period of ten years." The
young lady, "closely associated with the Black Panther
movement in New Haven," was shown Polaroid photo-
graphs of the mutilated body.

"That's Brother Alex"—she nodded. This unidentified informant was only the first of many to sing a willing and
sordid ballad of the events witnessed on Orchard Street.

(The identity of this initial informant was carefully guarded throughout the trials, though it is widely speculated she was a distraught lady friend of one of the men present. Her word alone was not enough.)

The crucial pinch of Frances Carter was made late that day in Bridgeport as she was leaving her factory job. Frances had been only an intermittent witness to the torture on Orchard Street and left, sickened, to go back to work. Finding herself under interrogation in New Haven police headquarters, she gave the statement on which police based their raid. The damaging nature of her statement did not come out until well over a year later. When Frances Carter testified as a "hostile witness" at the trial of Lonnie McLucas, she reluctantly recalled her description to New Haven police of the scene she witnessed in the bedroom on Orchard Street:

On Tuesday, May 20, " . . . The man was still on the bed covered partially by a blanket. He was moving at that time and Rose Smith, who was in the bedroom, told me that she thought infection was setting in. I did not stay in the room long, as the man had urinated in the bed and the room smelled bad. . . . I went downstairs and told Lonnie McLucas that I thought it was a terrible thing that had happened to the man, and he told me, 'Oh, he'll be all right,' or words to that effect. . . ."

(It was a statement which would come to haunt Frances Carter, especially when she was later called on to repeat it and to testify against her own sister, Peggy Hudgins. She refused. But police were ultimately able in court to justify raiding the Panther headquarters, without a search warrant, on the probable cause given by their known informant and *corroborated* by the Frances Carter statement.)

Shortly after midnight on Thursday, May 22, a heavily armed team of uniformed and plain-clothes officers smashed their way into Warren Kimbro's town house without a search warrant. They knew exactly where to look for everything. The exact drawer, for example, in which to find a stash of pot. Handcuffs were ready for Warren and the five young women found there, including Ericka Huggins.

Sirens ripped through the New Haven night. Relatives frantically phoned the precinct. Attorneys were routed from bed. But everyone was barred from the station house for twenty-four hours.

A handsome, agitated young black man tried everything he could think of to get past the detective bureau.

"I want to get in and investigate which party members have been arrested."

"Identify yourself," a detective demanded.

"Lonnie McLucas," the young man said, a breath short of surrendering.

The detectives—incredibly—sent him away. Lonnie drifted to Hartford, then to Baltimore and Jersey City and finally, halfheartedly, he set out for California to make a personal report to the party leadership.

Cockiness quickly shook out of the eight captives as they were shunted into interrogation rooms. Their faces, puffy with fatigue and the pinched, frightened eyes of caught children, were not seen until the next afternoon. Police had tipped off the local paper. Their faces were strung across the *New Haven Register* under a banner headline: 8 PANTHERS HELD IN MURDER PLOT.

They were given one-name identities: Carter. Smith. Wilson. Edwards. Hudgins. Kimbro. Huggins. Francis. The two stray girl children from New Jersey talked a scared blue streak and were released. Their tapes were labeled Juvenile A and Juvenile B. That was the last time they were seen around New Haven.

"How the hell were they going to be revolutionaries!" howled Betty Kimbro Osborne. Denied admittance to the precinct to see her brother, she had to wait for the next afternoon's paper for basic facts, such as who had helped whom to kill whom.

"What kind of disciplined revolutionaries have things so goddamned loose as to get involved in an offing with women and children—" Sobs of outrage choked off Betty's words.

But the one prisoner who continued through the next few weeks to exude a passionate confidence was Warren Kimbro. The party, he insisted, would take care of everything.

Sobs dried quickly in Betty Osborne's throat. The parched fury stayed and bitter gravel began to form deep in her stomach. Sickened by the naïveté that had been found in a local idealist and twisted into this grotesque outcome—*which she had foreseen*—Betty tried to find explanations. She visited her brother regularly. She clipped the papers compulsively. New names kept coming up: pregnant girls and mental midgets she had never heard of, the people who gave orders and the people who talked to police. The bitter gravel rose in Betty and each night she came home to spill it out.

"Everybody is worried about the conspiracy J. Edgar Hoover is pulling. I'm worried about the conspiracy that goddamn party is pulling against my brother! They took a local dude with *leadership ability,* a person who was well-established in the community, and he was used. He gave his life to the party. But since everybody got picked up there hasn't been a mention about Warren. He hasn't seen a Panther since! It's all Bobby Seale and Ericka Huggins. I really blame myself for what happened, for not nagging more. . . ."

The systematic dismantling of the Black Panther Party began in New Haven. From Warren Kimbro's apartment on Orchard Street, where white America detected a deadly virus, the national stool-pigeon network was turned on and anti-Panther vaccine went out. Federal agents raided chapters in Washington, D.C., Salt Lake City, Denver and Chicago, looking for Sams, McLucas, Williams and Hithe.

In June Lonnie McLucas, out of bread and hope in Salt Lake City, walked into a Western Union office. He was hoping to find a money order from party headquarters. FBI agents took him into custody instead. He asked to give a statement.

It was noted that the young fugitive spoke almost with relief: "I became disillusioned with the party because of the violence . . . wanted to quit . . . afraid to quit because I had learned too much . . . I was afraid I might be killed."

In a second formal statement to a New Haven police sergeant, Lonnie McLucas elaborated on a discussion in Ericka Huggins' kitchen; he said Bobby Seale was told by Ericka that "We have a brother from New York City being questioned" and that George Sams said that he had reason to believe Rackley was an infiltrator and had something to do with the Panther 21 bust in New York. McLucas then quoted Seale's reply that Sams would "deal with" Rackley because Seale himself "didn't have time to relate to nothing like that."

In early August George Sams heard in Canada that Toronto police were coming for him. He mentioned to a local officer that he was afraid of being killed in connection with a political assassination in New Haven. Then he sent for the FBI.

Three days later Bobby Seale was arrested in Berkeley, California, on a fugitive warrant and the implicating word of George Sams. By the end of August the raids that snowballed out of Orchard Street had crippled every national party leader. The Panthers were in jail, in exile or in coffins.

Fall 1969

Suddenly Warren Kimbro's letters to his sister no longer bore the stock Panther slogan as the signature.

All summer he had waited in Montville State Correctional Center for a word from the Panthers. No word came. From euphoria he languished into an emotional coma . . . jumpy, paranoid . . . stopped eating . . . dropped twenty pounds. He asked Betty to bring a book on her next visit: Karl Menninger's *The Crime of Punishment.* From prison authorities he requested Catholic literature. Raised a Catholic, he had dropped from the Church to embrace the Panther creed. Now, it seemed, a large abandoned evangelical void inside Warren Kimbro longed to be filled.

His letters began to come home signed simply—with his pet name and love.

December 1969

In Macy's, racing against the limits of a charge-plate Christmas, New Haveners had already forgotten. When Betty Osborne bumped into Mrs. Huggins, they spoke in a private shorthand. Propped on Mrs. Huggins' weary shoulder was Ericka's baby. Had Betty been to court for the bail hearing? Mrs. Huggins asked.

"No. Warren's not involved. Have you?"

Mrs. Huggins said no. She looked bent with the work of it all. There was pressure on her to bring the baby to court for ammunition. Every morning before going to work at Sterling Library, she dropped the baby off at a prenursery program. Saturdays she brought Mai up to Niantic for Ericka to see. But she didn't enjoy those visits, Mrs. Huggins confided. She and Mr. Huggins had been planning to retire. . . .

Betty Osborne tugged at a string on Mai's bonnet to make the leftover Panther baby laugh, and to keep the proud, private tears from breaking out of Mrs. Huggins.

"She's a lovely baby."

Mrs. Huggins said she was a happy baby. She hoped to keep her that way.

On December 29 Judge Palmer filed a memorandum in answer to the defendants' motion for bail six months before. Frances Carter had time in between to give birth and watch her baby taken away. The infant went to Frances' parents in Trumbull.

Happy New Year to all, and to all bail was denied. Except

for Frances Carter, who had given police the original statement. Her family posted $750 bond on her bail of $10,000.
But after six months in jail her freedom lasted all of forty-
eight hours. This time, subpoenaed to testify at a probable-
cause hearing, Frances refused to talk. Prosecutor Arnold
Markle invoked a brand-new immunity law, giving her a key
to her cell if and when she decided to talk her way out. Then
Judge Mulvey returned her to prison on a six-month contempt charge.

It was a new year. But the past weighed heavily on New
Haven. A decade that had begun with grand infusions of
money, talent and the promises of white politicians closed
with a torture, a murder and the promised spectacle of a
Black Panther trial. New Haven was like an old man who
had kicked up his heels in middle age and suddenly, mysteri-
ously, could not take the stairs anymore.

Looking back on the decade that had ended so bitterly for
America's Model City, people first asked, Why?

An uncomfortable conclusion about the decade of urban
renewal kept pushing up through the rationalizations: Citizen participation and urban renewal had never been accom-
plished *together* in an American city. Urban renewal
inevitably meant knocking down people's homes. Citizen
participation only mobilized around the people's fight to save
their homes. It might have been called more accurately citizen defense. (Without a threat as vital as the loss of their
homes, poor working people haven't the luxury of time for
self-government. Besides, politicians rarely consulted them
until "participation" was a matter of survival—the block
against the bulldozer.) Thus urban renewal produced citizen

participation that mobilized to defeat it. Quite possibly, the two were fundamentally incompatible. One thing was certain by 1970: both issues had been buried alive.

The particular tragedy in New Haven was timing. Because this chosen city had started earlier than her envious sister cities, the human lessons of the sixties came too late. By the time citizen defense mobilized and the concepts of "human renewal" and "people programs" emerged, New Haven's face-lift was three-quarters completed. The rest was on the drawing board. Still time enough to add pretty words. But too late to undo the blind, self-perpetuating bureaucratic motions of city planning tied to federal funding.

But if the men of vision had been able to see past their egos and edifice complexes, the Model City dream might have come at least partly true for both black and white citizens. It came so close in New Haven. When people could not find a simple explanation for the failed dream, they began to ask, Who? Who had let them down?

One man was a key. But by the time I met him in July of 1970, he was another victim of the New Haven tragedy.

9

FRED HARRIS had an official position at last. New Haven's original black militant, the founder of Hill Parents Association, he had been installed at Connecticut Mental Health Center as an ombudsman for the community. His name was still a household word. But it no longer appeared regularly in the local paper. Whatever political clout Harris and HPA finally achieved had been almost totally eclipsed by the Panthers.

"Freddy Harris?" It was just a whisper off the rumor pump that July. "We hear he's been hanging around a shooting gallery on Congress Avenue."

The name popped up in another startling form on a pathetic scare letter. Titled "Head of the Vanguard," the mimeographed letter had evidently been fired off to all black New Haveners who worked for the city Redevelopment Agency, accusing them of being "house folks." Most of the signatures belonged to recent ex-convicts. Among them, whether by choice or without his knowledge, was the name Fred Harris.

"They're using Freddy again," commented a community worker in the Hill section. She shook her head sadly. "Trouble with Freddy is he never learned how to refuse anyone."

Fred Harris is waiting for me on his lunch hour outside the sophisticated new plant of Connecticut Mental Health Center. He bounds into the car and picks up my copy of Gordon Parks' *A Choice of Weapons*.

"You're too radical for me," Fred Harris says. He laughs and I laugh, but our laughter cannot harmonize at this moment in history. His eyes are soft and strikingly vulnerable. He seems to know this and keeps his face turned toward the window. Dressed in a checked sport shirt and khakis, his small frame encloses an enormous condensed energy. The car vibrates with it. From the moment Fred Harris gets in, he never stops politicking.

"Haay, sister." He punches a fist out the car window. "Power!" While the light changes, he jumps out to kiss a Puerto Rican baby sitting on a stoop with his mother. It is one-thirty on Congress Avenue. The sidewalks are hot with July sun and full with the restless overflow of unemployed black men, the first to be fired in this or any recession. Fred seems to know everyone.

"Stop here, baby," he says, and dashes across the street to the Johnsonian café, which has metal grids over its windows. "Keep a watch," he calls. "The pigs'll think you're here to cop dope."

Ten minutes later Fred comes out with a paper cup of vodka. Rattling past him up the street is an open trailer truck piled high with junk. Split mattresses worm out of its slatted wooden sides. A young black boy without expression sits on top. Fred raises his fist and shouts, "Power!" This boy with dull eyes and bad teeth, riding through Congoland on a pile of trash, suddenly has something to smile for. He holds up both arms and grins. "Power!"

"Sorry about calling you baby," Fred says, sliding back into the car. "I call everyone baby." He hesitates. "Maybe we should have stayed in the office. People might get the idea I'm fooling around with a white girl. It could be very damaging." This from the man who once amazed everyone by his friendly tolerance in working with whites.

"How do you like your job at the Mental Health Center?"

"I created the job," he says. "The only reason was to find out how the place functions, how Yale and the state fit in, so when we talk about community control we know how to hit, where to hit."

The next is a dangerous question. "How do you get along with the Panthers?"

"Whenever I can be of help to the Panthers, I do what I can."

"Do they call on you?"

" . . . Occasionally."

The answer came hard and now Fred points to a drugstore where he wants to stop. Then he disappears into a rooming house next door. Back in the car his voice is suddenly furry. The memories of glory and pain loosen and begin flooding out of mental storage.

"It's frustrating. When my wife and I and Willie Counsel started Hill Parents Association, we politicized people for the first time. The difference between HPA and the Panthers is, we *did* what we said we would. The Panthers may be a better disciplined group. But HPA was a married group, with children. At least, we were all married in the beginning: . . ."

Fred's voice catches and he looks quickly out the window.

". . . By now the guys have all been through hell," he picks up. "We all have old charges against us—conspiracy, extortion, possession of narcotics. The pigs have us on the end of a stick. A lot of old-timers like me are getting divorced now."

Fred Harris dealt. From 1962, when he and his wife and friends formed Hill Parents Association, Fred dealt for black groups, Puerto Rican groups, low-income white groups—anyone who had a problem or a program that begged for a spokesman to carry it to City Hall. To young blacks Fred Harris was the local Martin Luther King, the hope. At the same time he worked for disfranchised whites and maintained his white contacts downtown. Fred was New Haven's first black ethnic politician. Although he behaved in the tradition of ethnic Irish and Italian politicians with which Connecticut was very familiar, he was not accepted. There was no tradition of *black* ethnic politicians. Fred Harris scared the Establishment.

His HPA group was small. A dozen men. They were easily ignored for the five years prior to New Haven's riot. Except by the police. When twelve young men in jackhammer boots went through a drill under the open windows of a schoolroom—for the benefit of police listening outside—they drilled like a hundred men.

"Brother Harris, Brother Counsel, Brother Johnson— march! Second line, march! Third line, march!"

And each time the same line with Brothers Harris, Counsel, Johnson and their few friends would bring their boots down under the open window. This very effective numbers game worked on the imagination of New Haven police.

Now, in the West Side Restaurant, Fred Harris pulls out a snapshot of three beautiful, high-chinned daughters and a small son. He stares a long while at the picture before passing it to me. His eyes fill up. Then a glaze like gelatin smears over the eyes and something in the back of the neck snaps. His chin drops.

Fred bounces back quickly. "Sorry, I have a little hangover. Let's see . . . So I took this job because I owe it to my family. They're getting older and they like nice things. My daughters are to the point where they want clothes to look pretty."

I had already been told that Fred Harris recently bought a house for his wife and children on a street full of play yards. He was living alone in a small apartment downtown.

"You see, I've been working with community groups for years now, usually without pay. Coming up, we didn't really deal with material things. Now my kids have a house. . . ." Fred slides a bit, then comes back strong. "People don't see my name in the paper as often, but they know I'm still behind things."

The next name to come up was Richard Lee. His fourteen years as mayor of New Haven ran concurrently, though

stormily, with Fred Harris' reign as the local black militant.
Fred scowls at the name. A shudder of unfinished rage goes
through his shoulders. I offer him a cigarette.

"Keep your cigarettes," he says. "Nobody buys Fred Harris. They couldn't buy me with a college education. All I had
to do was get out of town and they'd have bought me four
years of college anywhere in the country."

A new irony about this Model City struck me. Richard C.
Lee and Fred Harris, the two men who figured most promi-
nently in the decade of the dream, had a good deal in common. Both were born in a cold-water flat and limited to a
high-school education. Both did odd jobs around Yale as
boys and looked upon the institution and educated men with
awe. Both tried to learn from every situation.

Fred was born in 1937 and, like so many of his contemporaries, watched his father dutifully wait on table for Yale
dons. Later Fred's father became a night hospital orderly
and Fred worked as a technician in the lab of Yale–New
Haven Hospital. In 1966, at the age of twenty-seven, Fred
Harris ran for a seat in the state assembly. He ran not with
the hope of winning but of having a platform within hearing
range of the city planners to present the problems of his
voiceless inner-city constituency. The local press effectively
ignored his candidacy.

By contrast, when Richard Lee ran for alderman at the age
of twenty-three, he won in spite of his youth and back-
ground. Lee came out of the Irish ward pol tradition and that
was familiar to people. Thus when only twenty-three, he
established the makings of a political base. Not that his rise

to power proceeded directly from there. Lee spent ten years as the director of Yale's public-relations outlet and weathered the emotional effort of two unsuccessful mayoral campaigns before his will to rule prevailed.

By the middle of the sixties both Harris and Lee had surmounted their handicaps and had become respected political leaders of their people. But the power of office resided with Lee.

Well before the riot one of Lee's advisers designated Harris "a responsible radical" and urged the mayor to open communication lines with Harris and the Hill neighborhood group. Even the neighborhood police liaison respected him. James Ahern, then a young cop with striking white hair, was a familiar figure around the Hill. He was quoted as saying he had no quarrel with Harris' goals and was not put off by militancy. Despite these recommendations, Mayor Lee and company proceeded on the fixed notion that Fred Harris, wherever he appeared, meant trouble. The idea that any grass-roots black organization could and would run its own human-renewal program was either inconceivable or intolerable.

After the riot—which Harris and Ahern worked together to quell—all attitudes hardened. It came just when Richard Lee's renewal projects were in high gear and his reputation as a save-the-city mayor was at its peak. The riot dealt Lee's prestige a terrible blow. It put his talent team on the defensive. At the same time it established the *fact* of Fred Harris as a political presence.

Up to then Harris had only been ignored. Suddenly he and

his friends became the objects of constant harassment and arrests. Three months after the riot, police raided Fred Harris' apartment at dawn. They arrested him on charges of possession of heroin and a stolen typewriter. He was cleared of the typewriter charge, but the possession charge hung over his head—usefully from a police point of view—for the next three years. As a young and black ethnic politician before his time, Fred Harris had always operated with two strikes against him. But perhaps his greatest weakness was something else. Fred Harris was emotional. It became apparent to him too late in the game that the political formula calls for cold blood.

Now I ask Fred for his latest perspective on James Ahern: "Have things improved since Ahern was promoted to Chief of Police?"

"It's been worse!" Fred laughs ruefully. "The reason is, HPA *trained* Ahern. As a police liaison he'd ask to come down and talk to our group. We allowed it because back in '64 we thought we were slick, letting the police know exactly where we stood. Ahern would sit there discussing positions and asking how the police could create a better image—to make us think he was really sincere. My guys treated him as just another guy. We cursed him out, blew his mind a little. Meanwhile, Ahern was digging our style. How we did things and what guys were what . . ."

Fred's voice velvets down to inaudibility again. Sweat builds into dewy patches around his nose. His eyes roll up under the lids like the numerals on a speedometer. It is a pattern now. He nods out for a few seconds every fifteen minutes. Then a quick shake of the head and Fred is back. In between he loses his place.

"Sorry, I'm not concentrating."

"What are you on, Fred?"

"Had some vodka, smoked a little grass. Mostly it's lack of interest."

We take a walk down the side streets off Congress Avenue and Fred snaps to life. Smiling, waving the fist, kissing babies —gently—collecting complaints, he moves through the people with enormous political style. Fred Harris obviously knows his business. Black New Haven cannot afford to lose him. They have no leaders to spare. But it is a cruel thing that happens to black politicians. Their black constituents lean hard and have a short memory for favors. Meanwhile, white liberals look on black politicians with a naïveté of the highest expectations. Misguided by an idealism we never apply to our own politicians, white people somehow think that black leaders, who are only now learning the process, can skip steps and avoid the bribes, pass through the system without heeling wards at home and compromising with the conservative fringe in City Hall. We expect black leaders and black-power groups to emerge pure and uncorruptible—by some immaculate political conception. When they falter, white liberals are the first to feel betrayed.

The 1967 riot in New Haven baptized Fred Harris once and for all into real-life racial politics. He has been trying to forget the experience ever since. As the story is told around town, rioting broke out in the Hill section by some spontaneous combustion of heat, frustration and a cop–youth shooting. It spread like a forest fire. Children and old men were caught up in it. Looting unleashed more looting. Fred Harris and his HPA co-captain Willie Counsel were horrified. They walked the streets trying to talk people back into their homes and prevent arrests. But the streets were filling with shattered glass. And the people, finally even the whole Puerto Rican community, came out to see what was happening and were caught up.

Police closed in on the inner city. Cop by cop they went at it like a boil. James Ahern, not yet police chief, was monitoring operations from Fred Harris' HPA office.

"These people aren't going home," Harris warned Ahern. "If you really want to do something constructive, send in the Sanitation Department with brooms and shovels. It will keep the people busy cleaning the streets."

But the police lines turned back the sanitation trucks. That pulled the last membrane of sanity off the riot area and, some said and some later denied, police bullets ripped into the boil.

Now I ask Fred Harris what the riot did to him.

"When it turned into a police riot, Ahern asked me to go back in and quiet the people. I drove down with Willie Counsel. Walking along Dixwell, a shot whistled past my ear. Then a second one. Willie pulled me down. 'Those shots are for you, Freddy,' he yelled. I said that was crazy and kept walking."

But his friend Willie would not be put off. "Our unit is tight, Freddy. The pigs know it. The only way to beat us is to pick off the leadership." Willie pulled Fred into the car and they retreated to the HPA office to demand protection from Ahern.

"Your cops are shooting at me!" Fred reported in amazement. Ahern laughed and said he was nuts. Fred called the police officer a motherfucker. It was the old cozy push-pull banter from the days when Ahern hung around HPA.

"He knew what to say next," Fred recalls. "He told me the Puerto Rican mothers and children were unsafe in the streets."

Once more the two paladins rushed back to the center of action, armed this time with the name of an officer who would extend them civilian protection. As they arrived, police were railroading a brother into the paddy wagon. Fred Harris walked over to report to the officer in charge.

"Three cops grabbed me. They pinned both arms behind my back. Another one started kicking me . . . in the groin. Not the first time . . . it's a . . . a thing with white cops."

Here Fred's voice begins again to string out, like a record pulling against a weak battery. We have talked now for six hours. Something other than vodka has been sucking out his brain at precise fifteen-minute intervals. In a few seconds Fred Harris will be gone again. Then his mind will jump back and the voice, like a skipping record, will pick up fast and clear somewhere else. It is an old black tragedy. But I cannot remember when it was more physically painful to watch. What eternal abomination of the American soul has corroded this man of gentle spirit into a nearly burned out militant at the age of thirty-three!

He strains to finish his story. "I was crying. . . . Willie was

telling me all the time, 'The pigs are out to off you, get it?
. . . to off Fred Harris' . . . and I wouldn't let myself look
at it, I couldn't look at it. . . .' "

Fred nods out here.

A month after this conversation the well-known ombudsman's appeal on the old drug-possession conviction was
overturned. His black friends shrugged. His white liberal
pals made themselves scarce. On September 15, 1970, Fred
Harris surrendered to New Haven police and entered jail.

10

WARREN KIMBRO'S BROTHER on the Dade County police force had called Betty Osborne from Florida in December.

"What's going on up there?"

"Your law-enforcement buddies are messing up over black people again," Betty said, having no love for police in any form, including brotherly.

"Are you a Panther?" her older brother William demanded.

"Isn't everybody?" Betty was flippant without thinking.

Brother William didn't like it. He insisted Betty give Warren Kimbro his address. She reluctantly passed it on. Warren did write and when his brother visited Montville, Warren said things were clearer to him now.

"When I made my first statement I was only concerned with what I had done, that I had made a fool of myself in shooting Rackley. I wasn't thinking about what anybody else had done." (This came out in Warren's testimony.)

"Now do what you were raised to do," Warren's brother pressed him.

On January 16 the abandoned "Panther"—who had never officially become a Panther—changed his plea from "innocent" to "guilty of second-degree murder." The mandatory sentence in Connecticut for that crime is life imprisonment. Warren later agreed to testify for the state. This brought the wrath of the Panthers down on him, the inevitable charges of "Pig!" and "Traitor!" But Warren Kimbro has very little to gain.

Chairman Seale did not appear in New Haven until spring. He had been detained and been made even more of a rallying point by the Chicago conspiracy trial. But in April, almost a year after the shooting, the feds finally brought Seale, Mr. Publicity, to town. Cast in place, the opening in New Haven was hailed at last by *The New York Times* for the high political theater it was:

SEALE IS THE MAIN DRAWING CARD
FOR PANTHER RALLY IN NEW HAVEN

May Day Weekend

Excitement built for six weeks. A handful of Black Panthers were planning the first rally in town to demonstrate support for the New Haven defendants. Yale came apart at the seams with controversy and finally closed down. The Park Plaza Hotel filled up with newsmen. Wire-service reporters came prepared with riot helmets and specially designed lightweight gas masks. The Karmelcorn Shop was doing a brisk business in ice cream and joint papers.

Thousands of gathering white ralliers (including us) accepted the popular line that Panthers were being framed again. A week before the rally we walked into the black community, photographer David Parks and I. We had our baby ears pinned back.

Over at Yale Medical Center, working around the clock to monitor rumors, a leader of the Black Coalition scowled at the radio. Reports of an impending clash between student ralliers and police peppered the air.

"Hell no, I don't want them to bomb everything," the black leader snapped. "We haven't had a piece of it yet."

The Coalition had released a memo through their newspaper, *The Crow,* spelling out what kind of welcome they held for visiting white Panther-lovers:

> They cry "right on" but their purpose is not our purpose and their goals are not our goals. The truth in New Haven, as in most of the country, is that the white radical, by frantically and selfishly seeking his personal psychological release, is sharing in the total white conspiracy of denial against black people.

Doug Miranda, new captain of the New Haven Panther chapter, and Big Man, editor of the Black Panther newspaper, were working hard to bolster the decimated local Panther ranks. They had been around to the black high schools all week. Enthralled, the kids promised to strike and march in a body to the rally. That set off an alarm which spread like night sirens through the black grapevine. Mothers went to the schools fighting mad and made their position vis-à-vis the Panther plan indisputably clear.

"No black kids are going downtown. No black parents are going downtown. Furthermore, here is where the line is drawn between the black community and the Green."

Arnold Markle, the state prosecuting attorney, wasn't sure who posed the greater threat—visiting Weathermen or local white ethnics, who seemed to have bought up every gun in the state. Before the rally an interesting conversation reportedly took place between Chairman Seale and the prosecutor, in the presence of Seale's local attorney.

"I want that goddamned Doug Miranda sent away," Markle reportedly said.

"Power to the People!" Chairman Seale said.

"Look, Bobby, let's understand. You control your people, the Panther followers. I can control my people, the cops. I want those kids to go to school. You get Miranda out of their hair."

Seale reportedly admitted he had his own doubts about Miranda.

From wherever the control came, the children of the black community did not appear at the rally. Fifteen thousand overwhelmingly white college students did.

Quake! Panic! Connecticut in a funk! Four thousand men of the 82nd Airborne and 2nd Marines were flown from North Carolina to bases in surrounding states to await the holocaust. Brown trucks rolled into the city and spilled National Guardsmen on the streets. Long mute lines of little boys in weekend soldier uniforms hid behind unsheathed bayonets, forbidden to speak to the passing rabble. Finally, on the afternoon of the rally, the Guardsmen wedged into York Street, two blocks from the Green. Come and get it, baby!

President Nixon was preoccupied at the time with the invasion of Cambodia. But while Attorney General John Mitchell and Governor John Dempsey and Senator Thomas Dodd helped to prepare the climate for violence, Yale President Kingman Brewster watered the fuse. The university family came together in hundreds of meetings. Striking students and black faculty aired their bitternesses, discussed ways to monitor the upcoming trial and generally slugged out the more obvious aspects of racism in the spirit of dinner-table debate.

Speaking to his faculty, Kingman Brewster made his famous statement: "I am appalled and ashamed that things should have come to such a pass that I am skeptical of the ability of black revolutionaries to achieve a fair trial anywhere in the United States."

May Day opened, flowery, in the tingling sun like the magnolia blossoms in Branford College courtyard. Welcomes everywhere. Long tables were spread with brown rice and Familia. Ripe-bosomed coeds dished up a soul picnic for the incoming bedouins of the Woodstock nation.

Meanwhile, superefficient student marshals patrolled the campus, giving it the prepared aura of a big-city emergency room. There were rock bands. And signs. Signs to the People's First Aid Station. Signs to the john. Signs everywhere bearing the commandment: HELP THE PANTHERS KEEP THE PEACE.

On Saturday afternoon people covered the Green like crocuses, bathing in May sun. The speechmakers worked hard. But the crowd was less combustible than convivial.

"The trial in New Haven is a trial of whether or not there is anything left in this country worth defending." Tom Hayden's words stunned the crowd to attention. Visibly pained by having to walk a rhetorical tightrope over the dubious heads of his Panther hosts, Hayden went on to make great promises on behalf of his sprouting white-revolutionary crocuses.

"We have to make an all-out effort starting this summer in every town around, every factory and college, and turn the whole New England area into a giant political-education class—the last political-education class they will have!" He challenged strike-bound students to form white Panther brigades.

Abbie Hoffman interchangeably shilled grass, revolution and release from Whitemiddleclass Paralysis. " . . . The most oppressed people in America are white middle-class youth. . . . My brother is a Chinese peasant and my enemy is Richard M. Nixon. . . ." A pause here for the obligatory rally commercial: *Fuck Nixon! Fuck Nixon!* The crowd obediently stood to do the chorus for Abbie's one-minute Nixon spot. He rewarded them: "We ain't never, never, never gonna grow up. We will always be adolescents. . . . Fuck rationality. . . . We got the adults scared to fuck anymore 'cause they know they're gonna have long-haired babies!"

Coming down from his rant, Abbie barely remembered to put in a plug for the Panthers, whose rally it purportedly was. He set up the crowd like tenpins and bowled them over: *Free Bobby! Free Ericka!*

Doug Miranda picked it up and went for a strike. The young Panther from Boston prophesied: "We just may come back with a half a million people and liberate New England!"

Stirring . . . yet, immediately after the rally, the movement lost focus. A handful of political groupies—four dozen whites from schools of paperback Marxism and a few black students from Harvard and Cornell—massed across the street from the local jail. They seemed to be begging for a group snort of pepper gas. A lineup of police, under the walkie-talkie command of Chief Ahern, stood with hardware on hip. Expletives flew. Two blocks away National Guardsmen stood in ready phalanxes.

Suddenly—weird—along came these infuriated marshals from the local black community. Shouting "When you leave, we've got to live here," they found themselves fighting across an iron fence against black students. Fighting black Harvard students—dream kids, for godsake! Painful.

Walt Johnson, John Huggins' childhood friend, and other black Yale students shrank in disgust from the spectacle of white radicals running loose across the Green.

"Credit-card revolutionaries" Walt Johnson pronounced them. "In July they'll be hitching to California on Carte Blanche. In August they'll be sitting in Allied Chemical discussing the great rally they pulled off in May."

The Panthers found themselves *in the middle*. The cops were behind them and the white militants were on the other side of the fence.

Over a milkyface boy in a Columbia T-shirt, who was viciously brandishing a broom handle, rose the imposing hulk of an aide to Doug Miranda.

"I want to kill a pig," whined the boy with the broom handle.

"What you got in your pocket, a Yo-Yo?" hollered the Panther. "You think those cops are packing plastic bullets? Who do you think they see first? The black faces, got it, kid? All black faces look alike. Panther faces. What you think I got in my pocket, kid?"

Milkyface shrank into his Columbia T-shirt. The Panther slapped a hand on his pocket in a fake draw.

"I got a gun!"

Milkyface dropped his broom handle and ran. The Panther turned with a smile. For the spectators he pulled out his empty pocket lining.

"This is not the time!" the Panther hosts hollered through bullhorns, driving their VW bus all over town.

Unforgettable. A bizarre coalition of Panthers, black residents and Kingman Brewster, leading Yale's liberal elite, had saved the day. The Yale rally went down as a *good* political festival, just as Woodstock was the only *good* rock festival.

July

Summer came but the People's army did not. New Haven's adult black community zeroed in on another, more urgent trial: how to scrape through the recession and send their children back to school. The rumor pump went dry.

Scrawny rallies staged across the street from Superior Courthouse scarcely made TV dinner news. Abbie Hoffman presided over one. He was thrown to the ground with a fearsome karate block by a girl from the resident Women's Collective.

Beyond that New Haven, now under Mayor Bart Guida

and the old pre-Lee Democratic machine, was quiet. Indeed, the only riot during the summer erupted at Cozy Beach in East Haven. Italian against Italian in a three-day fire-setting melee over July Fourth. Embarrassing! Six men were arrested by Patrolman Joseph Pagano and Patrolman Nicholas Bencivengo. One of the Italian rioters was charged with assaulting an officer with a—yes—a motor vehicle. Really very embarrassing, yet an interesting counterpoint. The outcome of these arrests was somehow never reported in the *New Haven Register.*

11

The Trial

CONFRONTING THE PANTHER TRIAL, New Haven's legal family was haunted by Chicago's experience with an antic conspiracy trial. As one state official sized up the New Haven situation in June, "We couldn't get a death penalty on the Panther case if guilt was written in stone."

First problem: how to select a jury of peers for black revolutionaries.

"Twelve elderly, uptight conservative blacks on a jury could be the worst news the Panthers ever had," one officer of the court said. He was equally concerned with the prospect of sending *one* black juror back to the wrath of the ghetto. The problem is, many black residents of New Haven County are unregistered and therefore scantily represented on juror lists.

"So," this observer guessed, "we'll get a mixed jury and a political verdict. A compromise. If we can avoid another Fred Hampton situation, I think we can get this trial into focus."

State attorney Arnold Markle knew this town. A short, feisty man who speaks to the snap of his expandable watchband, he is anxiously liberal. Markle is quick to admit his home state has one of the most unprogressive criminal codes in the nation; he instituted classes to educate police officers on the rights of the accused. He has worked hard to abolish the death penalty and liberalize narcotics laws. But he was determined to break the hold of Panthermania on his town.

Markle was not about to let anyone from Washington get his hands into this trial and make a name for himself. Nor to let the defense get bad press to build a case of political persecution. He won a court order prohibiting "extra-judicial statements" by practically everybody connected with the trial, which lowered the voice of the press below a whisper.

What had begun with the arrest of seven political infants and a resident idealist, having already unleashed incredible racial combustion across the nation, came finally to public view fourteen months later. Now it was billed with all the really-big-show words in the indictment: conspiracy to murder, kidnapping resulting in death, conspiracy to kidnap, binding with intention to commit a crime.

Early local headlines did not improve the Panther image. Unfolding in newspapers dropped near the Dellwood milk box each morning were such improbable images as:

LISTENED TO RECORDS, SMOKED POT
AFTER SLAYING, SAYS KIMBRO

Stunned by bizarre testimony, New Haveners began to ask questions. Had this been the work of an efficient, nationally controlled paramilitary organization? Or was it simply Amateur Night in New Haven? Was Alex Rackley murdered by a chain of orders systematically handed down from the top? Or by nothing more than flailing egos of the rank and file in a fit of braggadocio?

It was hardly a proud moment for the Black Panther Party. Determined to protect Seale from a conspiracy rap, the party started out by heaping abuse on George Sams as a police informer. But the Panthers had a hard time making anybody, including their own lawyers, believe it.

Was Rackley "iced" on the basis of casually dropped kitchen rhetoric by Chairman Seale? Or because George Sams was desperate to ingratiate himself with his old friend Stokely Carmichael so that together they could take over the party (as the defense suggested)? Or, as the Black Panther newspaper had decided, because Sams was "a crazy bootlicking nigger . . . our diagnosis from the perspective of revolutionary psychiatry"? Or because George Sams was simply a desperate misfit who was himself afraid of being killed?

Chairman Seale, advised of Warren Kimbro's nonimplicating testimony, rejoiced: "That puts the state up shit's creek, doesn't it?"

But the party itself was ultimately moved to give a formal statement: "The Black Panther Party has to stand in judgment [by] the people, because in that period of our party's development, we allowed a maniac such as George Sams to come into our party."

The outcome of the New Haven Panther trial was determined by the first move in the chain of events leading to the trial.

There are no Panthers in Connecticut except Ericka, was

the declaration from national headquarters. When Landon Williams and Rory Hithe were dispatched to purge the East Coast chapters, the chain of paranoia and internal mistrust was set in motion. Now, in the Superior Courthouse of New Haven one year and three months later, the rule was: Every man for himself.

This was not to be any New Wave conspiracy trial. Politics would not come before people. Defense attorney Theodore Koskoff, an officer of the National Trial Lawyers Association, set out to prove the system could work, even for a black revolutionary. Providing he dresses nice and plays straight.

Each day the New Haven trial became less an exhibition of gross racism and political injustice, and more a Rabelaisian ballad of individual human desperation, fear and fallibility.

The jury was another crucial "actor" in the surprise ending of the first trial. To understand the personality of a New Haven County jury, it is important to cross the invisible line that separates the bustling city from the Valley. Most of the jurors and the large square pocketbooks that sit on their laps come out of the Naugatuck Valley.

The Valley and New Haven begin to divide where the Naugatuck River brushes the city on its south side. The river grinds up through central Connecticut under sensible iron-grid bridges, tracing the old water-powered artery of once-great mills and a metal industry. The Naugatuck is stony and shallow. Pinned to its banks are proud, homely nickel-and-dime towns—Derby, Ansonia, Shelton, Seymour, Waterbury, Thomaston—towns with sides made of imitation asphalt shingle, the dull red crusty sides of the old mills. For good reason, the people of the Valley are not quite living in this century.

When unions pressed too hard, the great metal monoliths like Anaconda relocated their facilities in the South. The Valley's dim-windowed mills and the skeletons of its metal works were left to pock and rot, offering little more than irresistible windows for schoolboys to break. People of the Valley, accustomed to working the bedrock of the state's economy, became narrow and hard with the piecework left to them. Finally speculators walked through the ruins. With a shrewd eye for capitalistic reconstruction, they began breaking up the mills and foundries into rentals for small-time manufacturers. Novelty items, shoes, hats, house dresses. And pocketbook factories.

The ladies who today "go down the pocketbook shop" to put together white vinyl with tin frames pass their lives gossiping about Hymie, the owner; they watch the world through David Frost and wait for jury duty. In 1970 they were brought by the hundreds to New Haven and selected to sit in judgment on the Black Panthers. Some of their husbands—the policemen and firemen and welders and tree surgeons—and their sons in the National Guard have never been to Hartford. But they are the law-enforcement pool for the state. And under the old county court system, these people provide the major juror pool for New Haven County.

A folksy group was chosen out of the 242 New Haven County electors examined on political and racial attitudes. The two black men, ten whites and one black woman alternate were chosen primarily for their parochial attitudes. The Panthers were to be judged by people who seldom if ever read about racial matters, much less about Panthers.

Careful, myopic, generally decent but mostly old, the jurors were finally seated. Propped on the women's knees like tea napkins, as a constant reminder of the behavior they would expect, were these square pocketbooks that come out of the Valley.

July 30

George Sams is doing a little singing in court downtown. In fact he is spilling the guts of the Black Panther Party all over the sidewalks of New Haven. The courtroom is small, orderly, square. Judge Harold Mulvey maintains a mild presence. There is no glare. Only a soft cosmetic whiteness that filters down from square, frosted ceiling lights.

George Sams enters to testify, cool as tap shoes. In his navy-blue blazer with padded shoulders, he swings within inches of the defense table to outface Lonnie McLucas on his way to the stand. Lonnie is dressed to perfection. But Sams is improving every day.

"Who's his tailor?" an attorney whispers to McLucas.

Another startling thing about the man whose IQ has been variously represented as 55 to 85: George Sams is an impressive witness. He gives intelligent replies. In fact, he is giving the defense a run for its money.

Now defense attorney Koskoff leads George Sams through an account of his travels over the three months following the murder. It's a dizzying journey.

KOSKOFF   You left Orchard Street in a car with Landon Williams and Rory Hithe, drove to Kennedy Airport and boarded a shuttle. Where did you go then?

SAMS   To Washington.

KOSKOFF   Landon wanted you to get records of Stokely Carmichael from a man named Jann in Washington, right?

SAMS   Yes . . . and to get the names of contacts who were counterrevolutionary to the Panther party so we could patrol the East Coast.

KOSKOFF   Did you get the records?

SAMS   No.

KOSKOFF   Did you get Jann's secretary?

SAMS   No.

KOSKOFF   As a matter of fact, the Black Panther Party never trusted you, right?

SAMS   No, they trusted me.

KOSKOFF   Didn't you tell Sergeant DeRosa that Stokely Carmichael was trying to take over the party?

SAMS   No . . .

While the jury is shuffled in and out of hearing range, the defense and prosecution haggle with George Sams over how many times he was expelled by the party—according to his own previously recorded statement. Judge Mulvey decides to hear the tape in his private chambers. Koskoff returns to pursue the same line, hoping to establish Sams' own mental imbalance as the singular motive for the murder. Meanwhile, Sams is demolishing the image of Panther party discipline. . . .

KOSKOFF　Weren't you afraid to come back to New Haven without the records and to tell Landon you didn't get them?

SAMS　Yes, a little afraid.

It is established that Sams hopped a taxi from Washington to New Jersey, then to "Mr. Krunstler's" office (attorney William Kunstler) in Manhattan, and the next day sped off for Chicago with Rory and Landon.

KOSKOFF　How'd you go this time?

SAMS　Mustang. (Murmurs of approval, in spite of themselves, come from Panther supporters in the spectator section.) We went to headquarters in Chicago to investigate the party policies and ideology.

KOSKOFF　How long did you stay in headquarters?

SAMS　Twenty minutes.

KOSKOFF　(Winding up in his starched collar to give this one everything he's got)　*It took you twenty minutes to investigate the party ideology?*

(He continues to lead Sams on his incredible journey. . . .)

SAMS　That Sunday we pulled out and went to the Panther houses in Detroit. There was a lot of problems going on there. National hadn't classified the chapter. We found a lot of renegades and counterrevolutionaries running around and it was clear to everybody there wasn't a total Panther in Detroit.

Bizarre. By Sams' account virtually every Panther chapter in America was suspect. Sams himself spent several days under house arrest in Chicago, then claims to have walked out with a .38 revolver one evening and passed, unrecognized, through a line of FBI agents surrounding the house. He fled to Canada disguised in a preacher's suit.

SAMS   I got my own place till I got captured. Somewhere roun' two and a half months later.

KOSKOFF   What were you doing in Canada?

SAMS   Running.

KOSKOFF   How did you live?

SAMS   People supported me. Some of them kids in SDS, the ones that split up over that Yugoslavia thing, and some people in the Communist party—they was all arguing with each other and supportin' me. Just a buncha liberals, you know.

The press section breaks up. Even the jurors snicker. The front line of Panther spectators is convulsed with laughter and the court, summarily, is recessed. *Just a buncha liberals* . . . Dynamite!

Recess. Lonnie's cousin from Port Chester is stretching his legs on the Green. He is a tall, friendly-looking man in his late twenties and the testimony has obviously knocked him out. Port Chester, he says apologetically, isn't hip to the Panthers yet.

"Man, I had no idea how widespread and powerful the party is," he says. He runs over the testimony from his point of view: George Sams hopping taxis to Jersey, jiving all over the country in planes and Mustangs, laying his hands on petty cash to go wherever he wants to go. What gets him—as it probably gets thousands of young men immobilized in dull jobs in dud towns—what really *appeals* about the Panther party (beyond its complicated political vision) is summed up in the final comment of Lonnie's cousin:

"Those cats do more travelin' than rich folks!"

The Movement is eating its last supper in New Haven. On the night of July 30, 1969, the People's army is ready to retreat. The eyes of the Bread and Roses coffeehouse are shut behind plywood windows. It is set to close tomorrow night. Inside, desultory trial-watchers and stragglers from the collectives—which never pulled more than two hundred people into the city at any one time—sit behind bowls of chlodnik and Familia. Not saying much of anything. Where were the promised brigades of white Panthers?

"As usual," confides a disillusioned summer radical, "the white revolutionaries are trying to do something good but they're messing it up. Worst part is how cruel they are. They have no humanitarian feelings for anyone outside the movement."

(Yale evicted the Panther Defense Committee from its storefront on Chapel Street in the middle of one July night. Next morning a truck had deposited the committee's possessions in the Liberation School down on State Street. Back around May Day, the PDC had been the focus of dedicated white Yale students. By July the whole committee was three people—two young angries led by a wimpy veteran of the spring trashing at Columbia.)

A tired, scholarly-looking young man drizzles into the booth beside us. He mentions he is from the Liberation School.

"Looks like you're about to close up, too," someone says.

"Tomorrow. Frustrated," drones the Liberation School organizer. "We couldn't organize the community. The workers wouldn't listen to us. The trial's a bore."

Slabammmmmmm! He blows in with chin whiskers and a loosely hung brown polo shirt. Packing a Nikon, the proverbial stranger, slapping back the old saloon door to set teeth once again on edge in the Bread and Roses coffeehouse.

"I'm a photographer for *Quicksilver Times*," he announces. "Just got in from Washington." He adjusts his mirror shades to glint us all straight in the eye.

The young man from New Haven's Liberation School slides him a handbill, recounting the week's trial proceedings. The *Quicksilver* photographer reads two, maybe three paragraphs.

"I'm speechless! How long has this mother trial been goin' on? What's the movement doing about this? Man, this is a really heavy city. You see a pig every ten seconds and they got these *green* lights on their cars. This is a fucking fascist state. I never seen a place that needs work so bad."

The Liberation School man comes briefly to life. "Did you

know the conspiracy against the BPP started with the raid here?"

"I dig," says the photographer. He lifts his polo shirt and flaps it around a little to cool himself off. While the Liberation School man goes into his political-education speech, the photographer is rolling a spitball out of the trial news.

"Yeaaaaah," exhales the man from *Quicksilver,* "I'm *serious* about staying in this city!" He leaps to his feet and hoists out the door, promising to return after he takes care of a little business.

Exactly ten minutes later, beaming, the photographer returns. "What a shot I got of Sams with a telephoto! Got him coming out of the courthouse, full face."

"You gonna stay around?" tests the Liberation School man.

"Well, I just met a cat on the street who says D.C. is really getting together."

"Yeah, and—"

"So maybe New Haven isn't the place to work. D.C. needs me, man."

That was about the level of commitment and duration of conviction brought to bear by the People's army on the liberation of New Haven last summer.

Lonnie McLucas smiled. The trial turned on that fact, which pretty much left revolutionary purists nothing to do but go home mad. Lonnie was every lawyer's ideal defendant: bright-eyed, boyishly handsome, a little shy, with an intelligent look about him and an irresistibly gentle manner. Furthermore, he was neat. Brass-buttoned-blazer neat. Stylish in his butterscotch shirt and print silk tie, impeccable

down to his British ankle boots. But not—how shall one say
—too *showy*.

They loved it. The square-pocketbook jury out of Nauga-
tuck Valley, fully assembled on August 11, was already in
Lonnie's pocket. Lonnie smiled at each one who smiled back.
He took notes.

It was pure theater! Lonnie McLucas was no sulky defendant. He was the director here, the LeRoi Jones of this
Broadway-tryout town, swiveling in his director's chair to
size up actors, audience, reviewers. Jotting notes toward the
final-script polish. Attorney Koskoff was the producer. He
wanted it played straight.

The jury spent thirty-three hours cooped up in a jury room
measuring fourteen by fifteen feet. In their hands was the
power to convict Lonnie McLucas for:

Kidnapping resulting in death—penalty: death.

Conspiracy to kidnap—maximum penalty: thirty years.

Binding with intent to commit a crime—maximum penalty: twenty-five years.

Conspiracy to murder—maximum penalty: twenty-five
years.

Grinning with delight, Lonnie McLucas emerged from the
courtroom on September 1 into a jubilant crowd of supporters. Together they saluted the verdict with clenched fists. The
young Panther had been acquitted of the first three charges
and convicted of conspiracy to murder, which carried the
lightest penalty.

The verdict seemed to please just about everybody. The
volatile past of Lonnie McLucas did not come out until the
time of sentencing. In addition to his felony conviction for

robbery, the old rape charge and the unsettled matter of a parole violation, Lonnie had broken out of a lockup two days before his New Haven trial began. It is interesting to speculate what effect these details might have had on jurors who were convinced Lonnie was the lost sheep who had wandered among wolves.

"Lonnie McLucas is a very gentle man," asserted one satisfied juror. "He's no detriment to society. It's his testimony that freed him, not his defense." But what the juror probably meant—the apparent key that unlocked a sympathetic response to this particular black revolutionary—was Lonnie's *delivery* of his testimony.

From the outset the New Haven trial was politically limp. But as an exhibition of the weaknesses inherent in any revolutionary organization, it was a very instructive trial indeed. The Black Panther Party here and across the nation faces two threats that have plagued their counterparts throughout history:

(1) *Rivalry for leadership.* The transfer of power within an elected party is generally orderly, and slow. By contrast, the followers of a revolutionary group instinctively look to their most extreme members for leadership. As a more militant warrior emerges to catch the imagination of the cause, the old leadership is impugned, attacked as weak, and either expelled or killed. By leaving the transfer of power to this turbulent process, a revolutionary party is always in danger of collapse through internal attack.

The fact is, Black Panthers are scorned by most other black-power groups, the Muslims in particular. The Muslims have an estimated sixty thousand members across the nation. They are constantly offering police in various cities confidential information concerning Panther activities. (It never appears in news reports because the Muslims have no interest whatsoever in dealing through white media.)

Members of US, the black cultural nationalist group, have killed at least four Panthers for which they have been prosecuted. Eldridge Cleaver, in sanctuary in Algeria, is regarded most dubiously beyond the Panther faithful. Many militants go by this rule of thumb: no black fugitive gets out of the country; he is *let* out of the country.

(2) *Informers and paranoia.* Informers, traditionally the government's most effective weapon against a rebellious party, serve two purposes. They provide information and induce the more devastating Infiltration Reflex. Innocents and hangers-on are suspected and tortured or killed in the manner of Alex Rackley.

As real and imagined informers build paranoia within the revolutionary cadre, the rebels begin turning one another in. Panthers have already testified against rival black militants. In New Haven they were being called upon to testify against each other.

There is one "revolutionary" organization in this country that beat the game. In its heyday the Mafia did not fool around with oaths and ideological loyalty. To belong you had to "make your bones." Kill somebody. With that tie, the Mafia had you forever. Joe Valachi was virtually the only public informer to slip out of the Mafia grip.

If the Black Panther Party, or its successor, decides to survive at all costs, it may have to copy the Mafia technique.

12

Beyond the Trial

THE MANSON TRIAL eclipsed New Haven through July. Our fickle media went for the traditional Hollywood-style sex–dope–murder trial. In early August New Haven paled again before accounts of the Marin County shoot-out. California again, but this time the California Panthers outdid themselves and surpassed most of the cherished desperadoes in American history for sheer theatrical–political virtuosity.

Jonathan Jackson and two armed companions literally stopped a trial dead. Taping a gun barrel to the judge's head, they posed for their own photographer, liberated two prisoners and spun off in a van with their hostages through rabid police lines into a kamikaze bloodbath. What's more, the guns were allegedly supplied by California's pet liberal heroine, the beautiful, brilliant and persecuted UCLA teacher under the electric Afro—Angela Davis. At first she vanished into the Ten Most Wanted list. At this writing, she awaits trial in a California prison, a trial which promises to be the chief courtroom event of 1971.

The Panther's newspaper took New Haven by the hand after the California courtroom shoot-out and explained the uses of public homicide and programmatic suicide:

> Every black person in this country must understand that which is happening in New Haven. Lonnie's railroad is almost over. We said at the beginning of the trial that the pigs would hurriedly in an unconstitutional manner try to convict Lonnie. This has happened. That is the main reason why brothers like Jonathan Jackson (etc.) are and were justified in their assaults on the pig judge, the racist jurors and the fascist police of Marin County.
>
> Revolutionary suicide [is] the new educational tool for the people!

Three thousand people poured forth from the Oakland community to salute the suicidal revolutionaries. Since John Huggins' death, the recruiting potential of a Panther funeral had increased tenfold.

"The Black Panther Party will follow the example set by these revolutionaries," prophesied Huey Newton in a riveting eulogy. "There is a big difference between thirty million unarmed black people and thirty million black people armed to the teeth. The high tide of revolution is about to sweep the shores of America. . . ."

Panthermania, of course, reignited New Haven. But the fires were quiet and hidden inside the children.

The trials drag on. With almost no notice Frances Carter, her sister Peggy Hudgins, George Edwards and Loretta

Luckes were given suspended sentences. Landon Williams and Rory Hithe remain in Denver, fighting extradition to Connecticut. Ericka Huggins and Bobby Seale have been in prison, denied bail, for a full two years since the day of Rackley's murder, while awaiting a trial that has only now begun. With its painfully antiquated and inequitable court system, the state continues to cook a violent stew.

Warren Kimbro will almost surely be called back to testify in the Seale trial. . . . Betty Kimbro Osborne will go back to sleeping fitfully on the living-room couch to keep her bitterness from poisoning her family. . . . Ericka Huggins, once the bold young symbol with raised fist on a Black Panther poster, will find many people have forgotten her name. And John Huggins' parents will look each day at the child, Mai. Tiny black girl-child in a berserk land—is she the orphan of a nearly burnt-out revolution? Is she the symbol of a hard-won pride? Or is she the promise of a future race war in which single human beings must be sacrificed for the collective political point?

Post-Panthermania

Abbie Hoffman phoned Mentor Jones in early August. His father answered.

"No," William answered. "My son would definitely *not* be interested in going to Cuba on a Yippie action."

When Mentor came home from a rap session at Number Nine, the local storefront drug-rehab center, his father had the suitcases packed. They went for a two-week forced holiday to the Jersey shore. The boy's corners softened. His first year as a preppie in Massachusetts had left Mentor feeling like a pound of plaster of paris, stained Oxford brown. Disillusioned with popcorn radicals, he had given up on trying to organize his movement through Massachusetts prep schools. He had come home to take the cure at Number Nine for the month of July.

All messed up. Smoking in the crash pad, surrounded again by rich white powdered baddies, Mentor realized he had been taken in as the token black head. He withdrew. The vacation in Jersey actually looked good. Mentor took along the great works of twentieth-century philosophy—Nkrumah's Handbook, *Rubin's* Do It, *the* Constitution of the Communist Party of China *and Rap Brown's* Die Nigger Die.

On the Sunday father and son returned, Mentor found the round black neighbor women still sitting next door on a tiny cement stoop. Sitting deep in their Sears webbed nylon chairs, still tying bows on their little girls' pigtails, sitting all day making fun of their men on a piece of the world no bigger than a closet. Mentor freaked.

"You're plastic people!" he jibed. "You're all caught up in the middle-class value cycle, going to work every day to jobs you hate for money you can't keep. Everything is based on money. If you can get your thirty thousand a year, fuck the other guy. If you can do it, he can do it. But everybody *cannot* do that. Cause the system is not set up that way."

The eyes of the round black women ran up and down Mentor as though he were an upstart weed.

"Listen heuh, *Mistuh* Mentor Jones," one neighbor woman said, rocking back on her Sears chair. "There's *one* way of tellin' how much of a man a man is. That's by how much money he makes."

Mentor decided not to waste his breath on the neighbors anymore. It was not quite the time. But he did make the decision to forget prep school. They needed him badly in New Haven. He knew it now! His calling was to organize local high schools into a third revolutionary force.

Looking Ahead . . .

NO LOITERING—ALL VISITORS MUST REGISTER IN PRINCIPAL'S OFFICE

September 1970. David Parks and I are looking for Mentor in a suburban New Haven high school which is suffering from shell shock over the drug explosion.

"Can you lay some hash on me?" a pale kid of about fourteen asks David. It is a funny note, because at the same moment, in this standard Greek-Revival-cum-green-lockers suburban high school filled with yearbook-picture kids, the old school band is whupping up a sports rally in the gym.

Badoom, badoom, babababababababaBOOM? The big tuba sound is rolling down the hall into the pit of the stomach and hundreds of bleached-jean boys are following girls in valentine-fanny pants and everybody—almost everybody—is tripping over clog sandals to get to the gym. The scene inside is pure 1950s. Bleachers stacked with white faces. Twirlers in Sunoco-gold serge and sequins flash pink knees at the letter-sweater boys. And the cheerleaders, all blond and busty, put forth the glossed-lip ideal of Miss Rheingold contestants.

Six black students sit in the bleachers. This is despite the jump in black enrollment to about one hundred and fifty students this year. Many have enrolled through the busing program. For five hundred dollars a black student can commute out of the inner city for an education in white suburban values. But where are they?

"They don't believe in the sports program," says one of Mentor's friends, falling into step beside us. "They don't believe in ———— High School."

Mentor is meeting with potential revolutionaries in the cafeteria. The unaffiliated of 1970 are out front waiting for school buses: the black bus children, standing apart, and the white hippies and heads, personified by two boys sharing an inhalator. A school mother stops to ask them directions. They answer politely, but without missing a sniff of happy powder from the inhalator.

Mentor comes from his meeting with an elbow folded around his blue notebook. A broad smile escapes him. A little showing off for his New York friends—his blazer, the YIP button, the hobo bandanna tied around his denim knee —and the frivolity is over. Mentor becomes again the solemn revolutionary moving on to the next step.

"Are you glad to be back at ———— High?"

"For one reason." Mentor works up his most ferocious stare. "To blow up the place."

Nine strong students, that is all Mentor needs to form his new party: RYM III, or Revolutionary Youth Movement to the third power (since SDS claims RYM I and II).

"It's an underground operation," Mentor says. "I want to keep it small so we can split quickly."

Rain is slapping hard against the windshield and we are driving home with a boy as desperate to claim his manhood as was John Huggins or Warren Kimbro. Mentor has stopped going to the flicks. All propaganda. High-school sports, he says, are for token blacks. Dope?

"Grass and acid, smack and coke—they're smoking it, popping it, swallowing it, I guess they're sniffing it, too." Mentor sounds bored. "I'm not into that. No time. I've been writing the manifesto for my new party."

"Hey, Mentor," David presses him. "Are you really going to blow up that school of yours?"

With us Mentor can drop his crazy act and be more honest.

"Symbolically speaking," he says.

We stop at Hungry Charlie's, a hangout near Yale where Mentor likes to be seen. Yale is the power base. To organize the local high schools Mentor needs Yale radicals to back him up. They pass our table: a familiar face from the December 4 movement at Columbia and a few Panther supporters of immense cool, who nod at Mentor with barely a dip of their gold-rimmed shades. But they only nod. Walter Dallas, who directs Yale's Black Ensemble Theatre Company and first encouraged Mentor to write plays, stops to ask what his former protégé is up to. Mentor says he spent the summer doing political work. Walter Dallas, a busy and elegant man, drops a casual invitation to Mentor to join a workshop and then moves on.

Frustration! By the surviving Panthers and his Yale heroes and even by the square white counselors down at Number Nine, Mentor is still being handled with a sort of fond, head-patting, come-back-next-year-kid friendliness. Mentor glowers over his horn rims.

He begins to recite from his own student manifesto: "We,

the Youth International Party, RYM III, do not advocate the use of drugs but we do recognize the national symbol, the black flag with the red star and the marijuana leaf up front—"

Mentor consults his blue notebook, which by now has grown fat and stringy with use. The cover hangs open to reveal a new secret pouch—a scrap from his father's old fatigues. It is filled with the forbidden books he now lives by. The pouch is inscribed in large letters: THIS REVOLUTIONARY'S NOTEBOOK BELONGS TO MENTOR JONES. The boy bends to read from his manifesto:

> There is a definite need to abolish the educational system as it exists today. The educational system is the indoctrination of students into a society that is class-antagonistic, racist, and economically exploits its people. It should be made clear the student is not actually learning but being fed facts like a computer, is not being trained to utilize these facts to benefit himself, but to aid a dying society. The black student in particular is given a 12-year course in servility.

"Here, you can read it." Mentor passes over his notebook, suddenly restless. In the margin a note from Mentor to himself catches the eye:

> Remain cool. Mentor, do not become emotionally violent when you make your presentation, or you will blow everything.

"What happens if someone finds your notebook now?" we ask.

"I kill myself."

We go separate ways in the afternoon.

At home the phone is locked. (William found too many calls to Chicago and Oakland and Abbie Hoffman on the phone bill.) But there is a rifle in the cellar now. An old .30-caliber Japanese carbine his father brought home from World War II. Mentor is still clumsy with it. Yet between the boy and the rifle in his cellar a certain friendship is developing.

"I've got to buy a book on guns," Mentor tells us in the cellar. On the sofa bed, with the rifle between his knees, he is picking its rusted innards out of an oil can and turning them over in his hands. He has the look of a boy who has lost his innocence.

"Take it easy," David Parks says.

"I'll stay alive," Mentor says. Then, brightening: "Hey, the next time you come up I'll be running rallies like Abbie Hoffman. That's what I'm training myself for."

"Keep in touch, Mentor Jones," I say, holding out an uncertain hand.

Mentor stands up stiffly, arms pasted to his sides. The mask begins to crumble like papier-mâché. For an instant his face is stripped raw of poses, theories, words, defenses and pretense—everything falls away except the loneliness of being fifteen and black in New Haven, Connecticut. Mentor bolts forward and drops a kiss on my cheek.

Tip-tick. Tip-tick. Upstairs with Mentor's father we sit late into the evening, listening as one listens for a fever to break. The *tip-tick* seems louder this time. And we share now with William the burden of knowing the difference between the sound of a pen and the sound of a gun.

"Does Mentor have his notebook down there with him?"

"I don't believe so," his father says. "He lost it this afternoon."

Mentor lies in the cellar working it out in his head. He has incorporated both the white radical experience and the black revolutionary reality. The Panthers are already passé to him —a party racked with internal killings and external police raids, exposed in courtrooms and belittled in his own town. Walking around inside his head now are three men who passed through early stages of Panthermania.

John Huggins died from it. Fred Harris was passed over by it, embittered, and finally sought escape in drugs. Warren Kimbro went to prison for it.

Jail holds little fear for boys like Mentor. It is, after all, only an extension of everyday humiliations and comes to be expected. More difficult to deal with now are the flirtations with martyred death. The nascent man of fifteen can be quick to squander his life, too quick. But Mentor is beginning to gain more accuracy in measuring the price of black manhood. He is more calculating than his predecessors. He does not plan to be killed cheaply.

Along with his contemporaries Mentor is struggling through to his own form. A volatile mix of the black and white revolutionary styles, it will lead to actions we cannot explain by simple cause and effect. It is a form which none of us—not William, Abbie, Bobby Seale, the white liberals, nor the black neighbor ladies—have seen before. In the end we are only listeners.

About the Author

Gail Sheehy has been writing and reporting for ten years. From the Rochester *Democrat & Chronicle Tribune* she joined the news staff of the New York *Herald Tribune,* and went on to become a free-lance contributor to many magazines, among them *New York, McCall's, Holiday,* and *Cosmopolitan.* As a contributing editor to *New York* magazine, she has gained a reputation for tough-minded personalized reporting of contemporary crises. Her first book, *Lovesounds,* was a novel. She has recently completed a fellowship in Interracial Reporting at Columbia University, from which *Panthermania* grew. She is also the author of a new paperback collection of her articles, *Speed Is of the Essence,* the title story of which will be released as a film by M-G-M this summer.

71 72 73 74 10 9 8 7 6 5 4 3 2 1